NEW ENGLAND
PIONEER PANTRY

COOKBOOK
COMMITTEE MEMBERS

Goldie Morrow—Chairperson
Janet Gavin—Co-Chairperson
Al Felenchak—Coordinator
Andy Gaunt—Artist
Nancy Stanley—Typist
Lynne Brooks, Debbie Poole, Sue Martineau
Paula Brown, Jean Warner, Carlene Godwin
Brian Major, Diane Andersen, Ladonna Maldonado
Art Contest Winner: **Pat Labelle**
Title Contest Co-Winners: **Diana Benson, Chris Kasila**
Cover Photo Credit: **Ray O'Brien**

PIONEER PANTRY DEDICATION

The Future Pioneer Cookbook Committee dedicates Pioneer Pantry to our Co-Chairperson, Janet Gavin. Janet's leadership in the planning phase of this project provided the momentum to see this cookbook through to completion. Her boundless energy, creative ideas, and endless drive are characteristics we all strive for as Future Pioneers. Recently, Janet experienced a physical setback which temporarily kept her away from work and this project. The Futures miss her contributions and look forward to her speedy and healthy return.

This cookbook is a collection of our favorite recipes,
which are not necessarily original recipes.

Published by: Favorite Recipes® Press
P. O. Box 305142
Nashville, TN 37230

Copyright© Merrimack Valley Works Chapter #78
Telephone Pioneers of America
1600 Osgood Street
North Andover, Massachusetts 01845

Printed in the United States of America
First Printing: 1991   12,500 copies

Library of Congress Number: 91-24078
ISBN: 0-87197-309-X

TABLE OF CONTENTS

RECIPE CONTRIBUTORS

Tom Abar
David Abbot
Mitch Abbot
Sari Abbot
Willis Abbot
Monica Allen
Steven Belair
Karen Belfiore
Luanne Berube
Louise Bistany
Claire Blades
Norma-Jean Blanchet
James Bodine
Kara T. Bodine
R. Louis Bodine
Theresa Bolduc
Gail A. Boucher
Carol Bowles
Cecele Brackett
Paula Brown
Theresa J. Burnham
Alice M. Cable
Karen Casey
Diane Champagne
Peggy (Chippie)
    Chapinski
Tud from Chicago
Cathy Collins
Andrea Consentino
Dianne Coppola
Shirley Cossar
Charlotte Curtis
Evon Danus
C. M. Demers
Anna DiMauro
June Dion
Anna F. Dodier
Marcy Dunton
Laura D. Durling

Kelly Eckbreth
John Evans
Joyce A. P. Fard
Irene Farrell
Betty R. Felenchak
Louise Filomeno
Barbara Flanagan
Arthur A. Foucault
Teresa M. Gagnon
Marie Gallant
Denise Gaunt
Sarah Gearlds
Kathleen A. Giacobbe
Sandra Girard
Rafael A. Gonzalez
Christine Green
Maria Green
Barbara A. Guerin
Claire Guy
Sue Hardy
Donna Hart
Norma Heaton
Jerre Holmes
Patricia (Colburn)
    Howes
Marie Jenkins
Maryjane Krepper
Terry Kyrlos
Barbara Lapinskas
Marie Laplante
Anna Lavoie
A. L. Levesque
Alice Litwinovich
Claire Lord
Brenda Major
James Major
Ladonna Maldonado
Margie March
Donna Martin

Susan Martineau
Edith McAllister
Elizabeth McNally
Adrian Melling
Goldie Morrow
Bob Pacini
Millie Pellegrino
Kathy Pothier
Millie Potter
Mary Prenaveau
Ralph J. Reed, III
Irving Reval, Jr.
Grace Riccio
Gina Rossetti
Beverly Ruel
JoAnn Runions
Annmarie Russo
Rene Russo
Nancy Salvage
Herb Sayers
Linda Searcy
Ron Searcy
Anne Seremet
Dee Smith
Ida Spaulding
Betsy St. Jean
Nancy Stanley
Patricia Stewart
Theresa Straw
Bonnie Stupak
Debborah Szczypinski
Helen Tabbi
Pat Tait
Claudia Trembley
Irene Vinci
Jean Warner
Anna Welch
Karen Wunderlich

4

WHO ARE THE "FUTURE" PIONEERS?

Just who are the "Future" Pioneers? Well, you may have heard of the Telephone Pioneers of America. It is the world's largest voluntary association of industrial employees, composed of telephone workers with 15 years or more service. The Future Pioneers are a branch of the Telephone Pioneers of America designed expressly for those employees with less than 15 years of service. The only requirement for membership is a desire to volunteer time and energy in serving special organizations within the community.

At the AT&T Merrimack Valley Works in North Andover, Massachusetts, the Future Pioneers are a chartered segment of Chapter 78, Telephone Pioneers of America. The Merrimack Valley Future Pioneers are welcome to participate in local Pioneer activities such as Feed the Needy, Special Olympic Field Games, Veteran Hospital Visits, and the Clown Troop, to name a few. However, the "Futures," as they are affectionately called, concentrate their efforts on their own projects.

The Futures organize an Easter Egg Hunt and a softball game with the St. Ann's Children's Home in Methuen, Massachusetts. St. Ann's is a state-run refuge for emotionally or physically abused children. Monthly, the Futures' Bingo team heads north to the Rockingham Country Nursing Home in Brentwood, New Hampshire for fun and fellowship. This activity culminates in a year-end Christmas Party, with plenty of gifts for all. The Futures enjoy their time with members of the Haverhill, Massachusetts Girls' Club giving a cookout/pool party and attending *Disney on Ice*. The Futures latest project is "Kids on the Block," a traveling life-sized handicapped puppet awareness show for children.

To help support these activities financially, the Futures also coordinate fund-raisers. These include the annual Future Pioneer Car Wash, the Cookbook of the Futures, and this Pioneer Cookbook.

Energy, enthusiasm, ideas, talent, and drive: These are the hallmarks of the Future Pioneers. Through the efforts of the Futures, the true Pioneer traditions of fellowship, loyalty and service are passed along to a broader spectrum of the telephone employee body. Their activities encourage understanding and relationships among all employees, enable community service, and provide opportunities for development and growth. Most of all, being a Future Pioneer is FUN!

KIDS HAVING KIDS
CHRISTMAS PARTY

The Future Pioneers hold a Christmas Party for teenage mothers who are in a counseling program run by the Sisters of the Holy Family Hospital in Methuen, Massachusetts. The Holy Family counselors help the girls deal with some of the problems they face in parenting at an early age. They provide parenting education, guidance, and emotional support.

The Christmas Party put on by the Futures aims at making the holiday season a little brighter. Gifts are given to the moms and their children, and Santa pays a visit.

FUTURE PIONEER COOKBOOKS

In 1990, as a fundraising project, the Future Pioneers put together a limited edition homemade cookbook called the *Cookbook of the Futures*. Based on its success, the Future Pioneer Cookbook Committee was chartered to develop this *Pioneer Pantry* cookbook as a major fundraising project for the whole Merrimack Valley Pioneer Organization.

The Cookbook Committee solicited recipes from fellow employees and retirees at Merrimack Valley. The recipes ranged from Appetizers to Main Dishes to Desserts. Proceeds from sales of *Pioneer Pantry* will go to fund Pioneer Activities.

CLOTHE OUR NEEDY NEWBORNS

This Future Pioneer Project provides layettes, that consist of handmade donations and purchased items, to the area hospitals. These donations are knitted and/or crocheted items. The Future Pioneer Organization supplies all of the yarn needed by volunteers to make these items. Each of these layettes is given to area hospitals where they are given, from the Future Pioneers, to needy families who remain anonymous to the Futures.

HANDICAPPED PUPPETS

The Handicapped Puppet Team teaches adults and children what it is like to be handicapped through the eyes of a puppet. The puppets each have a disability unique unto itself which include Cerebral Palsy, blindness, deafness, mental retardation, learning disability, and Downs Syndrome.

The Future Pioneers will support a few teams, of two volunteers each, who will learn and perform pre-written skits to area schools and activity groups. The puppets' size and imaginative clothing and accessories make them appear to be alive as they talk to each other and field questions from the audience. Children of all ages learn that it is okay to ask handicapped members of the community about their disabilities. If you love children and have a secret dream to be on stage, then this team is for you.

HAVERHILL GIRLS' CLUB

Two activities are held annually for the Haverhill Girls' Club. A cookout/pool party in August and a special field trip in February.

The Annual Cookout/Pool Party is held at the home of Mr. and Mrs. Donald Gavin, in Newton, New Hampshire. Approximately 60 young females are in attendance for this event. They are supported by six Girls' Club staff members and the volunteers from the MVW Future Pioneers. A full August day is filled with challenging games and activities, swimming, special events, and a wide variety of foods and refreshments for the children's enjoyment.

In February, the girls are taken to a special event in the Boston area. This year's activity, Walt Disney's "Disney on Ice," combined both the excitement of a live entertaining show and the pleasure of seeing some of the most popular and loveable animation characters. Again, six staff members support approximately 60 young females. In their role as chaperons, the Future Pioneers are able to provide special attention to each of the young ladies and also that extra margin of safety in movement throughout the activity.

SPECIAL OLYMPICS

The Special Olympics Field Games for handicapped persons are held every spring. Local special-needs persons are invited to participate in such games as relay races, frisbee and softball toss, soccer ball kick, and other field events. These games are held to create a greater understanding by the general public of the needs of special people and at the same time, offer these people the opportunity to experience the pride and satisfaction that can come through competition. The games are tailored to fit the contestant's capabilities, and this fun-filled day concludes with an awards ceremony and trophy presentation.

ST. ANN'S HOME

St. Ann's Home is a residential center for children with special behavioral and emotional needs. The home is well staffed with a psychotherapist and a staff nurse. The schooling that these children receive is equivalent to a special needs program that is offered in public schools. The children who come to the home are put in units that only contain up to thirteen children. The staff-to-child ratio is about one to four.

The first social event for these children is the Annual Easter Egg Hunt and Holiday Party. The children love the attention and have a fun time on the Saturday before Easter. Volunteers and clowns support and work with the children who are busy finding the eggs that the volunteers have hidden. The enthusiasm and laughter of the children puts a smile on everyone's face and makes the day complete.

The second event is a softball game with the Futures playing against the children of St. Ann's. There will be other types of games going on for the smaller children. Following the game we serve pizza and tonic to all. This is fun!!!!

ROCKINGHAM COUNTY NURSING HOME

The Future Pioneers, in conjunction with other groups, such as the Pioneers, Retired Pioneers, and the Friends of Pioneers, gather monthly to provide a warm and friendly atmosphere for the Rockingham County nursing home patients, located in Brentwood, New Hampshire.

On the first Wednesday of every month, the Pioneering organizations coordinate BINGO for the patients at the nursing home. This activity utilizes volunteer support for calling, writing called numbers on the blackboard, setting up, handing out prizes, and assisting patients to play the game.

The annual special event is a Christmas Party at which each patient is treated to an evening of music, song, and celebrating the holiday. Each member is given presents or other surprise gifts. The Strummers are there to entertain as well as a special visit by Mr. & Mrs. Santa Claus. The patients are given holiday foods and beverages which are preplanned in accordance with their individual diets.

Some love and support is all that is needed to maintain the spark in anyone's heart.

FEED THE NEEDY

As part of the community involvement of Merrimack Valley Works Chapter #78 of the Telephone Pioneers of America, we proudly participate in the "FEED THE NEEDY" program. We sponsor and serve a meal at the Haverhill Senior Citizen Center in Haverhill, Massachusetts, on the third Monday of each month. Over 200 people are served, including many homeless. In Lawrence, Massachusetts, we support the Lawrence Daybreak Shelter, a haven for the homeless, throughout the year. We have an ongoing Canned Goods Drive, and distribute this food to many organizations in the Merrimack Valley area.

HOSPITALIZED VETERANS PROJECT

In December of 1987, Officers of the Thomas Sherwin Chapter 14 and the Merrimack Valley Works Chapter 78 proposed that the "National Salute to Hospitalized Veterans" held during Valentine's week each year be adopted as a project of Region 12. This proposal was accepted and since then, many of the chapters of Region 12 have expanded their activities at the VA Medical Centers throughout New England.

In the accompanying photo, Chapter 78 Pioneer clowns, Rainbow and Fluffy, entertain and salute a patient at the Manchester, New Hampshire VA Medical Center.

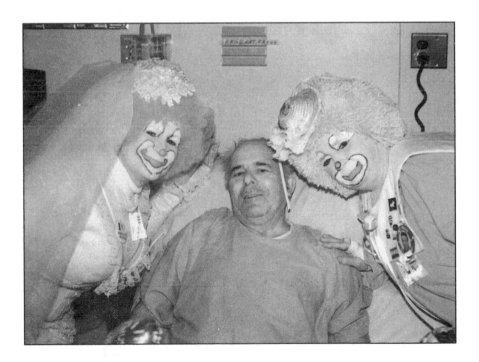

AUDIO BALL

The Audio Ball is a sound-equipped ball that blind people can catch, bat and use to play baseball. It is a regulation-size softball with a beeping sound module in it. Before the module is inserted, the ball is partly unstitched and a hole is drilled. The mechanism is then fastened into place and the stitches resewn. The unit is powered by Nicad batteries and is rechargeable. Originally designed for a blind youngster to use, the project has progressed to the point where an Audio Ball World Series is held each year, with participant teams from throughout the United States. A recent program on the Today Show featured the assembly operation and highlights of last year's World Series in Chicago, Illinois. In 1972, the Merrimack Valley Works Chapter set up an assembly line to mass-produce the balls. It is staffed by a group of Life Members, who devote one morning a week to the project. Our Life Members can turn out about 30 to 40 units a week.

THE PIONEER STORE

A major undertaking by the Life Members of the Merrimack Valley Works Chapter #78 Telephone Pioneers of America is helping at the Pioneer Store. The Pioneer Store is open one day a week for the employees of AT&T. It is our main source of revenue for the charity fund. The Pioneer Store offers our employees a variety of products, with good quality and affordable prices. It has also proven to be a great social event, as retirees and employees renew acquaintances and generate new ones.

The Store Committee is made up of both active and retired Pioneer Members.

PIONEER CLOWN TROUPE

The Telephone Pioneers of America, Chapter 78's clown troupe is looking for volunteers. A few hours a month is all that is needed. The clowns visit area nursing homes with the musical group called the Strummers.

They work with the elderly, the veterans, the handicapped, the terminally ill, and the disabled.

In 1988 they did a total of 78 events for a total of 3,315 volunteer hours.

There is no age limit and no service limit to be a clown. Everyone is welcome. When you join, you may bring along your spouse, your child, mother, father or a friend. Makeup sessions and balloon sessions are provided, as well as guidance in your choice of costume and clown name.

We will stand by to help at all times until you are ready to stand alone. We can promise you will receive more pleasure from being a clown than you could possibly give.

You are cordially invited to join our clown family.

APPETIZERS
AND BEVERAGES

Sugar House
Mendon, Vermont

PINEAPPLE CHEESE BALL

Yield:
45 servings
Utensil:
bowl

Approx Per
Serving:
Cal 73
Prot 1 g
Carbo 2 g
Fiber <1g
T Fat 7 g
Chol 11 mg
Sod 172 mg

16 ounces cream
cheese, softened
1 8-ounce can
crushed pineapple,
drained
1/4 cup finely chopped
green bell pepper

2 tablespoons finely
chopped onion
1 tablespoon seasoned
salt
2 cups chopped pecans

Combine cream cheese and crushed pineapple in bowl; mix well. Add green pepper, onion, salt and 1 cup pecans; mix well. Shape into ball. Roll in remaining 1 cup pecans to coat. Chill, wrapped in foil, for several hours or overnight. Serve on tray with assorted crackers.

THREE-CHEESE BALL

Yield:
45 servings
Utensil:
bowl

Approx Per
Serving:
Cal 104
Prot 4 g
Carbo 1 g
Fiber <1 g
T Fat 9 g
Chol 24 mg
Sod 137 mg

16 ounces cream
cheese, softened
16 ounces sharp
Cheddar cheese
1 5-ounce jar blue
cheese

1 tablespoon wine
vinegar
Garlic salt to taste
1 cup chopped walnuts

Combine cream cheese, Cheddar cheese, blue cheese, wine vinegar and garlic salt in bowl; mix well. Shape into ball. Roll in walnuts to coat. Chill until serving time.

CREAMY CHILI CON QUESO DIP

Yield:
100 servings
Utensil:
casserole

**Approx Per
Serving:**
*Cal 42
Prot 2 g
Carbo 1 g
Fiber <1 g
T Fat 4 g
Chol 10 mg
Sod 44 mg*

8 ounces extra sharp
   Cheddar cheese,
   shredded
2 4-ounce cans whole
   chili peppers,
   chopped
3 cups sour cream

8 ounces mild
   Cheddar cheese,
   shredded
8 ounces Monterey
   Jack cheese,
   shredded

Alternate layers of 1/3 of the sharp Cheddar cheese, chili peppers, sour cream, mild Cheddar cheese and Monterey Jack cheese in 2-quart casserole until all ingredients are used. Bake, uncovered, at 375 degrees for 30 minutes or until hot and bubbly. Serve hot with corn chips. This reheats well.

CUCUMBER DIP

Yield:
40 servings
Utensil:
bowl

**Approx Per
Serving:**
*Cal 61
Prot 1 g
Carbo 1 g
Fiber <1 g
T Fat 6 g
Chol 9 mg
Sod 48 mg*

8 ounces cream cheese,
   softened
1/2 teaspoon hot
   pepper sauce
1 cup mayonnaise
2 medium cucumbers,
   seeded, chopped

2 tablespoons chopped
   green onions
1 tablespoon lemon
   juice
2 tablespoons (or
   more) dillweed

Combine cream cheese, hot pepper sauce, mayonnaise, cucumbers, green onions, lemon juice and dillweed in bowl; mix well. Chill until serving time. Serve with vegetables.

TESSIE'S NUT ROLL DIP

<table>
<tr><td>

Yield:
50 servings
Utensil:
bowl

Approx Per Serving:
Cal 54
Prot 1 g
Carbo 2 g
Fiber <1 g
T Fat 5 g
Chol 10 mg
Sod 27 mg

</td><td>

1 15-ounce can crushed pineapple, drained
16 ounces cream cheese, softened
1 medium green bell pepper, finely chopped

</td><td>

1 small onion, finely chopped
1 cup finely chopped walnuts
1/2 apple, finely chopped

</td></tr>
</table>

Combine pineapple and cream cheese in bowl; mix well. Add green pepper, onion, 1/2 cup walnuts and apple; mix well. Shape into ball. Roll in remaining 1/2 cup walnuts to coat. Chill for 2 to 3 hours before serving. Serve with Ritz crackers or potato chips.

SHRIMP DIP

<table>
<tr><td>

Yield:
64 servings
Utensil:
gelatin mold

Approx Per Serving:
Cal 41
Prot 2 g
Carbo 1 g
Fiber <1 g
T Fat 3 g
Chol 17 mg
Sod 71 mg

</td><td>

1 10-ounce can tomato soup
3 ounces cream cheese, softened
1 teaspoon unflavored gelatin
1/4 cup water
1 pound cooked shrimp, chopped

</td><td>

1 medium onion, chopped
1/2 cup chopped green bell pepper
1/2 cup chopped celery
1 cup mayonnaise

</td></tr>
</table>

Bring soup to a boil in saucepan. Add cream cheese, stirring until dissolved. Soften gelatin in water. Stir into soup mixture until dissolved. Add shrimp, onion, green pepper, celery and mayonnaise; mix well. Pour into mold. Chill until set. Unmold onto serving dish. Serve with crackers.

SCRUMPTIOUS SHRIMP DIP

Yield:
16 servings
Utensil:
bowl

Approx Per
Serving:
Cal 22
Prot 2 g
Carbo 1 g
Fiber 0 g
T Fat 1 g
Chol 15 mg
Sod 41 mg

1 4¹/₄-ounce can tiny
  shrimp, drained
¹/₄ cup shrimp and
  seafood sauce
¹/₄ cup plus 2
  teaspoons sour
  cream

Combine shrimp, sauce and sour cream in bowl;
mix well. Serve with assorted crackers.

LAYERED TACO DIP

Yield:
90 servings
Utensil:
serving dish

Approx Per
Serving:
Cal 22
Prot 1 g
Carbo <1 g
Fiber <1 g
T Fat 2 g
Chol 5 mg
Sod 35 mg

8 ounces cream cheese,
  softened
1 cup sour cream
Garlic powder to taste
Pepper to taste
1 small onion, chopped
1 medium tomato,
  chopped
1 8-ounce jar salsa
¹/₄ cup chopped olives
1 cup shredded lettuce
1 cup shredded sharp
  Cheddar cheese

Combine cream cheese, sour cream, garlic powder
and pepper in bowl; mix well. Spread in square
serving dish. Layer onion, tomato, salsa, olives, lettuce and cheese over cream cheese mixture. Chill
until serving time.

MEXICAN DIP

8 ounces cream cheese,
  softened
1 cup sour cream
1 envelope taco
  seasoning mix
1/2 head lettuce,
  shredded

1 medium tomato,
  chopped
1 small onion, chopped
1 12-ounce jar
  picante sauce
8 ounces Cheddar
  cheese, shredded

Combine cream cheese, sour cream and taco seasoning mix in bowl; mix well. Spread in 8x10-inch
serving dish. Chill for 1 hour. Combine lettuce,
tomato, onion and picante sauce in bowl; toss to
mix. Spread over chilled cream cheese mixture.
Sprinkle with cheese. Chill until serving time. Serve
with nacho chips.

TEX MEX PARTY DIP

3 medium avocados,
  mashed
1/2 teaspoon salt
2 teaspoons lemon
  juice
1/4 teaspoon pepper
1 cup sour cream
1/2 cup mayonnaise
1 envelope taco
  seasoning mix
2 10-ounce cans bean
  dip

1 cup chopped green
  onions
3 medium tomatoes,
  chopped, drained
2 3-ounce cans
  chopped olives,
  drained
8 ounces sharp
  Cheddar cheese,
  shredded
2 12-ounce packages
  tortilla chips

Combine avocados, salt, lemon juice and pepper in
bowl; mix well. Combine sour cream, mayonnaise
and taco seasoning in bowl; mix well. Layer bean
dip, avocados, sour cream mixture, green onions,
tomatoes, olives and cheese on large serving platter.
Serve with tortilla chips.

TASTY NONFAT DIP

Yield:
30 servings
Utensil:
bowl

Approx Per
Serving:
Cal 12
Prot 1 g
Carbo 2 g
Fiber 0 g
T Fat <1 g
Chol 1 mg
Sod 75 mg

2 cups nonfat plain
  yogurt

1 envelope ranch
  dressing mix

Combine yogurt and dressing mix in bowl; mix well. Chill for 1 hour or longer. Serve with assorted fresh vegetables.

SUMMER FRUIT DIP

Yield:
40 servings
Utensil:
serving bowl

Approx Per
Serving:
Cal 47
Prot 1 g
Carbo 7 g
Fiber 0 g
T Fat ? g
Chol 6 mg
Sod 22 mg

8 ounces cream cheese,
  softened

1 12-ounce jar
  marshmallow fluff

Combine cream cheese and marshmallow fluff in serving bowl; mix well. Serve with strawberries, pineapple and grapes to dip. May layer with slices of angel food cake and fresh fruit for dessert.

CREAM CHEESE SPREAD

Yield:
40 servings
Utensil:
serving bowl

Approx Per
Serving:
Cal 27
Prot 1 g
Carbo <1 g
Fiber <1 g
T Fat 2 g
Chol 17 mg
Sod 54 mg

8 ounces cream cheese, softened
1 onion, chopped
2 hard-boiled eggs, chopped
1/4 cup chopped olives

Combine cream cheese, onion, eggs and olives in serving bowl; mix well. Chill until serving time. Serve with assorted crackers.

JOHN GIACOBBE'S CHEESE FONDUE

Yield:
20 servings
Utensil:
fondue pot

Approx Per
Serving:
Cal 155
Prot 10 g
Carbo 3 g
Fiber <1 g
T Fat 9 g
Chol 31 mg
Sod 90 mg

6 cups shredded Swiss cheese
1/4 cup flour
2 1/2 cups white or blush wine
2 tablespoons sherry
Garlic powder to taste
Pepper to taste
Nutmeg to taste

Combine cheese and flour in bowl; toss to coat cheese. Pour wine in fondue pot. Heat until air bubbles start to rise. Do not cover. Do not boil. Add cheese, a small amount at a time, stirring until melted and smooth. Add sherry, garlic powder, pepper and nutmeg; mix well. Serve hot with French bread cubes, apple chunks, Vienna sausage or fresh vegetables.

RICH CHEESE PUFFS

Yield:
65 servings
Utensil:
baking sheets

Approx Per Serving:
Cal 61
Prot 2 g
Carbo 2 g
Fiber <1 g
T Fat 5 g
Chol 21 mg
Sod 88 mg

1 cup butter, softened
6 ounces cream cheese, softened
2 eggs, beaten
1/4 teaspoon hot pepper sauce
2 cups finely shredded Cheddar cheese
1 1/2 cups flour
1 teaspoon salt

Combine butter and cream cheese in bowl; mix well. Add eggs and hot pepper sauce; mix well. Add cheese, blending well. Stir in flour and salt. Chill for 30 minutes. Roll dough 1/2 at a time on generously floured surface to 1/4-inch thickness. Cut with 1 1/2 to 2-inch cookie cutter. Place on baking sheets. Bake at 375 degrees for 12 to 18 minutes or until edges are brown, rearranging baking sheets once while baking. Remove to wire rack to cool.

BEST-EVER CHICKEN WINGS

Yield:
24 servings
Utensil:
baking pan

Approx Per Serving:
Cal 118
Prot 10 g
Carbo 4 g
Fiber <1 g
T Fat 7 g
Chol 28 mg
Sod 706 mg

1   10-ounce bottle of soy sauce
2 teaspoons grated fresh ginger
3 cloves of garlic, minced
1/3 cup packed brown sugar
1 teaspoon dark mustard
24 chicken wings
Garlic powder to taste

Combine soy sauce, ginger, garlic, brown sugar and mustard in bowl; mix well. Wash chicken; pat dry. Separate chicken wings at joints; discard tips. Spread chicken in shallow baking pan. Pour marinade over chicken. Marinate in refrigerator for 2 hours; drain, reserving marinade. Bake at 350 degrees for 1 1/2 hours, turning and basting with reserved marinade frequently. Sprinkle with garlic powder. Cook under hot broiler for 1 to 2 minutes or until brown.

Chinese Chicken Wings

<table>
<tr><td>

Yield:
20 servings
Utensil:
baking dish

Approx Per
Serving:
Cal 105
Prot 9 g
Carbo 1 g
Fiber <1 g
T Fat 7 g
Chol 28 mg
Sod 93 mg

</td></tr>
</table>

½ cup barbecue sauce
2 tablespoons
  Worcestershire sauce
¼ cup duck sauce

2 tablespoons Ah-So
  sauce
20 chicken wings

Combine barbecue sauce, Worcestershire sauce, duck sauce and Ah-So sauce in bowl; mix well. Wash chicken; pat dry. Separate chicken wings at joints; discard tips. Place chicken in baking dish. Baste with sauce. Bake at 350 degrees for 30 minutes. Turn chicken; baste with sauce. Bake for 30 minutes longer.

Nutritional information does not include duck sauce and Ah-So sauce.

Chili Chicken Wings

<table>
<tr><td>

Yield:
12 servings
Utensil:
baking sheet

Approx Per
Serving:
Cal 344
Prot 26 g
Carbo 15 g
Fiber <1 g
T Fat 19 g
Chol 79 mg
Sod 246 mg

</td></tr>
</table>

½ cup apricot
  preserves
¼ cup chili sauce
1½ teaspoons
  chopped onion
2 cloves of garlic,
  minced
½ teaspoon celery salt

½ teaspoon chili
  powder
¼ cup packed brown
  sugar
¼ teaspoon pepper
3 pounds chicken
  wings

Combine apricot preserves, chili sauce, onion, garlic, celery salt, chili powder, brown sugar and pepper in saucepan. Cook over low heat until mixture bubbles, stirring occasionally. Wash chicken; pat dry. Separate chicken wings at joints; discard tips. Spread chicken in shallow dish. Pour marinade over chicken. Marinate for several hours in refrigerator. Place chicken on baking sheet. Bake at 350 degrees for 20 minutes. Turn chicken. Bake for 20 minutes longer. This marinade is also good on leg of lamb.

CONFETTI PIZZA

Yield:
15 servings
Utensil:
baking sheet

Approx Per Serving:
Cal 313
Prot 4 g
Carbo 15 g
Fiber 1 g
T Fat 27 g
Chol 33 mg
Sod 458 mg

2 8-count cans crescent rolls
12 ounces cream cheese, softened
1 cup mayonnaise
2 tablespoons dillweed
1½ cups chopped broccoli and cauliflower flowerets
1 large tomato, chopped
1 small purple onion, chopped
1 4-ounce can chopped olives
1 carrot, shredded

Unroll crescent rolls. Separate into rectangles. Roll out on floured surface to fit 10x15-inch baking sheet, sealing perforations. Place dough on baking sheet. Bake at 400 degrees for 10 minutes. Cool to room temperature. Combine cream cheese, mayonnaise and dillweed in bowl; mix well. Spread on cooled crust. Combine broccoli, cauliflower, tomato, onion, olives and carrot in bowl; toss to mix. Spread over cream cheese layer, pressing lightly into cream cheese. Chill until cold. Cut into squares to serve.

CRAB MEAT ENGLISH MUFFINS

Yield:
72 servings
Utensil:
baking sheet

Approx Per Serving:
Cal 34
Prot 1 g
Carbo 2 g
Fiber <1 g
T Fat 2 g
Chol 7 mg
Sod 105 mg

½ cup butter, softened
1 5-ounce jar Old English cheddar cheese spread
1 tablespoon mayonnaise
½ teaspoon seasoned salt
½ teaspoon garlic salt
1 7-ounce can crab meat
6 English muffins, split

Combine butter and cheese spread in bowl; mix well. Add mayonnaise, seasoned salt and garlic salt; blend well. Stir in crab meat. Spread on English muffin halves. Freeze for 10 minutes. Cut into sixths. Place on baking sheet. Cook under hot broiler until brown.

HOT DOG APPETIZERS

Yield:
160 servings
Utensil:
saucepan

Approx Per Serving:
Cal 23
Prot 1 g
Carbo 1 g
Fiber <1 g
T Fat 2 g
Chol 3 mg
Sod 89 mg

2 10-count packages hot dogs
1 14-ounce bottle of catsup
1 12-ounce can beer
3 tablespoons (or more) brown sugar

Cut hot dogs into 1-inch slices. Combine hot dogs, catsup, beer and brown sugar in saucepan; mix well. Simmer for 30 to 40 minutes, stirring frequently. May be served hot or cold. Chill overnight to enhance flavor.

SWEET AND SOUR KIELBASA

Yield:
12 servings
Utensil:
saucepan

Approx Per Serving:
Cal 143
Prot 3 g
Carbo 23 g
Fiber <1 g
T Fat 5 g
Chol 12 mg
Sod 365 mg

1 16-ounce kielbasa
1 teaspoon vinegar
1 12-ounce jar apricot jam
2 tablespoons dry mustard
2 tablespoons soy sauce
2 tablespoons vinegar
1 8-ounce can pineapple chunks, drained

Combine kielbasa, vinegar and water to cover in saucepan. Simmer for 20 minutes. Remove kielbasa; cool to room temperature. Combine apricot jam, mustard, soy sauce and 2 tablespoons vinegar in saucepan. Bring to a boil. Add pineapple. Cut kielbasa into slices. Add to sauce. Simmer for 15 minutes, stirring occasionally. Serve hot.

MARINATED MUSHROOMS

1 pound mushrooms
1 clove of garlic,
    minced
1 small onion, thinly
    sliced
1/2 teaspoon oregano

1/4 teaspoon paprika
1/2 cup oil
1/2 cup wine vinegar
1/4 teaspoon pepper
1/2 teaspoon salt

Steam mushrooms in boiling water in saucepan for 1 minute; drain. Rinse in cold water; drain. Combine garlic, onion, oregano, paprika, oil, vinegar, pepper and salt in bowl; mix well. Add mushrooms. Marinate, covered, in refrigerator for 24 hours; drain before serving.

STUFFED MUSHROOMS

1 pound large
    mushrooms
1/2 small onion,
    chopped
1/4 cup margarine
8 Townhouse crackers,
    crushed

Parsley flakes to taste
Pepper to taste
1/4 cup grated
    Parmesan cheese
1 egg, beaten

Cut stems from mushroom caps; chop into fine pieces. Sauté mushrooms stems and onions in margarine in skillet until onion is tender. Add cracker crumbs, parsley flakes, pepper, cheese and egg; mix well. Stuff into mushroom caps. Place in baking pan. Cook under hot broiler until golden brown.

PRAWN COCKTAIL

Yield:
4 servings
Utensil:
glasses

Approx Per Serving:
Cal 207
Prot 14 g
Carbo 5 g
Fiber 1 g
T Fat 14 g
Chol 129 mg
Sod 266 mg

1 egg white, beaten
1 tablespoon chopped parsley
1/4 cup shredded lettuce
8 ounces cooked prawns or shrimp
1/4 cup mayonnaise
1 tablespoons catsup
2 tablespoons whipping cream
1 tablespoon Irish or Scotch whiskey
Dash of Tabasco sauce
8 thin slices lemon
8 thin slices cucumber

Dip rims of 4 champagne glasses into egg white; dip into parsley to coat. Layer lettuce and shrimp in glasses. Combine mayonnaise, catsup, cream, whiskey and Tabasco sauce in bowl; mix well. Spread over shrimp. Cut into lemon and cucumber slices at halfway point. Place on rim of glasses.

PARTY MIX

Yield:
24 servings
Utensil:
baking sheet

Approx Per Serving:
Cal 103
Prot 2 g
Carbo 15 g
Fiber 2 g
T Fat 5 g
Chol 7 mg
Sod 42 mg

4 cups bite-sized shredded wheat cereal
1/2 cup mixed nuts
1/2 cup shredded coconut
1/3 cup butter
1/4 cup frozen orange or pineapple juice concentrate
2 tablespoons honey
3/4 teaspoon ginger
1 cup raisins

Combine cereal, mixed nuts and coconut in large bowl; mix well. Combine butter, orange juice concentrate, honey and ginger in saucepan. Cook until butter melts, stirring frequently. Add raisins. Cook for 2 minutes or until raisins are soft, stirring frequently. Add to cereal mixture; toss to coat. Spread on baking sheet. Bake at 350 degrees for 12 to 15 minutes or until cereal is light brown, stirring once. Cool to room temperature. Store party mix in covered container.

PARTY SNACK

Yield:
20 servings
Utensil:
baking sheet

Approx Per Serving:
Cal 295
Prot 3 g
Carbo 24 g
Fiber 1 g
T Fat 23 g
Chol 26 mg
Sod 120 mg

20 saltine crackers　　**2 cups chocolate chips**
1 cup butter　　**2 cups crushed walnuts**
1 cup sugar

Line baking sheet with foil. Arrange crackers to cover baking sheet. Combine butter and sugar in saucepan. Cook until frothy, stirring constantly. Pour over crackers. Bake at 350 degrees for 5 minutes. Sprinkle with chocolate chips. Let stand at room temperature for 5 minutes. Spread chocolate over crackers; sprinkle with walnuts. Cut into servings at edge of crackers. Chill in freezer for 20 minutes. Let stand at room temperature for 3 minutes. Remove from foil.

PEACHES AND CREAM LIQUEUR

Yield:
6 servings
Utensil:
blender

Approx Per Serving:
Cal 299
Prot 5 g
Carbo 33 g
Fiber <1 g
T Fat 12 g
Chol 109 mg
Sod 73 mg

1/2 cup plus 2 tablespoons sweetened condensed milk
1　5-ounce can peach nectar
1/2 cup whipping cream
1/2 cup peach brandy
1/4 cup orange flavored liqueur
2 eggs
1 teaspoon vanilla extract

Process condensed milk, peach nectar, whipping cream, brandy, liqueur, eggs and vanilla in blender container for 1 minute or until smooth. Chill, covered, in refrigerator. Will keep for 1 month in refrigerator. Process in blender or shake before serving.

Piña Colada Punch

Yield:
20 servings
Utensil:
punch bowl

Approx Per Serving:
Cal 146
Prot 1 g
Carbo 10 g
Fiber <1 g
T Fat 6 g
Chol 0 mg
Sod 9 mg

1¹/₂ cups canned cream of coconut
3 cups pineapple juice
1¹/₂ cups crushed pineapple

24 ounces club soda, chilled
1 pint light rum, chilled

Combine cream of coconut, pineapple juice and pineapple in pitcher. Chill, covered, until very cold. Pour into punch bowl. Stir in soda and rum just before serving.

Slushy Fruit Fizzes

Yield:
9 servings
Utensil:
freezer container

Approx Per Serving:
Cal 107
Prot 1 g
Carbo 27 g
Fiber <1 g
T Fat <1 g
Chol 0 mg
Sod 6 mg

6 ounces frozen pineapple juice concentrate
1¹/₂ cups orange juice
1¹/₂ cups water

1 tablespoon honey
1 banana, mashed
1 liter lemon-lime tonic

Combine pineapple juice concentrate, orange juice, water, honey and banana in 9x13-inch freezer container; mix well. Freeze until firm. Scoop into glasses just before serving. Add lemon-lime tonic to fill glasses.

SOUPS
AND SALADS

Lobster Feast
Damariscotta River Campground
Maine

Autumn Soup

1 pound ground turkey
2 large onions,
   chopped
6 carrots, sliced
6 stalks celery, sliced
6 cups water
1 16-ounce can
   tomatoes
6 low-sodium beef
   bouillon cubes
1 cup corn
1 teaspoon basil
2 bay leaves
2 ounces barley
Salt and pepper to
   taste

Combine turkey, onions, carrots, celery, water and tomatoes in large stockpot. Bring to a boil. Add bouillon cubes, stirring until dissolved. Add corn, basil, bay leaves, barley, salt and pepper. Simmer for 1 hour or until carrots are tender, stirring occasionally. Remove bay leaves. Ladle into soup bowls.

Cream of Broccoli Soup

1 bunch broccoli, cut
   into spears
2 large potatoes, cut
   into 1-inch cubes
4 carrots, thinly sliced
1 large onion, chopped
2 stalks celery,
   chopped
2 cloves of garlic,
   minced
2 tablespoons chopped
   fresh parsley
2 tablespoons oil
2 chicken bouillon
   cubes
4 to 5 cups water
3 to 4 cups milk
8 ounces Cheddar
   cheese, shredded
1/2 teaspoon salt
1/2 teaspoon pepper

Combine broccoli, potatoes, carrots, onion, celery, garlic and parsley in large stockpot. Add oil, bouillon cubes and water. Bring to a boil. Simmer until bouillon is dissolved and vegetables are tender, stirring occasionally. Remove from heat. Remove broccoli to bowl. Purée soup 1/4 at a time in blender container. Return soup to stockpot. Add milk to desired consistency. Stir in cheese until melted. Add salt, pepper and broccoli. Bring to serving temperature. Ladle into soup bowls. Garnish with parsley.

CREAM OF BROCCOLI AND CHEDDAR SOUP

Yield:
6 servings
Utensil:
stockpot

Approx Per Serving:
Cal 540
Prot 12 g
Carbo 14 g
Fiber 2 g
T Fat 50 g
Chol 140 mg
Sod 331 mg

1 bunch broccoli
1/3 cup chopped onion
6 tablespoons margarine
1/4 cup flour
2 cups whipping cream
2 cups milk
4 ounces white Cheddar cheese, shredded
Salt and pepper to taste

Steam broccoli over boiling water in steamer until deep green. Sauté onion in 2 tablespoons margarine in stockpot until tender; drain. Melt remaining 1/4 cup margarine in stockpot. Add flour, stirring to mix. Stir in cream. Simmer until thickened, stirring constantly. Stir in milk gradually. Simmer until soup is desired thickness, stirring constantly. Stir in cheese until melted. Chop half the broccoli into bite-sized pieces. Purée remaining half in food processor. Add salt, pepper, broccoli and onions to soup. Simmer for 10 minutes, stirring frequently. Serve with French bread.

CAULIFLOWER SOUP

Yield:
12 servings
Utensil:
stockpot

Approx Per Serving:
Cal 207
Prot 5 g
Carbo 21 g
Fiber 3 g
T Fat 12 g
Chol 9 mg
Sod 561 mg

2 cloves of garlic, minced
1 small onion, chopped
4 to 5 tablespoons chopped salt pork
1/2 cup margarine
1 10-ounce can chicken broth
2 broth cans water
3 chicken bouillon cubes
4 medium potatoes, cubed
1 large head cauliflower, chopped
Pepper to taste
1 tablespoon chopped fresh parsley
1/2 cup half and half
1 tablespoon lemon juice

Sauté garlic, onion and salt pork in margarine in stockpot until onion is tender. Add chicken broth, water and bouillon cubes. Simmer until bouillon is dissolved. Add potatoes. Simmer, covered, until potatoes are tender, stirring occasionally. Add cauliflower, pepper and parsley. Simmer for 5 minutes. Reduce heat. Stir in half and half and lemon juice, mashing ingredients to thicken soup.

CHEESE SOUP

1/2 cup chopped onion
1/2 cup chopped carrot
1/2 cup chopped celery
1 teaspoon finely minced garlic
2 tablespoons butter
1/3 cup flour
2 teaspoons cornstarch
3 cups chicken stock
8 ounces Stilton cheese, crumbled
8 ounces Cheddar cheese, shredded
1/8 teaspoon soda
1 cup whipping cream
1/3 cup dry white wine
Salt to taste
1/8 teaspoon cayenne pepper
1/4 teaspoon black pepper
1 bay leaf
1/4 cup chopped parsley

Sauté onion, carrot, celery and garlic in butter in 4-quart saucepan until soft. Stir in flour and cornstarch until well mixed. Stir in chicken stock. Simmer until thickened, stirring constantly. Stir in Stilton cheese and Cheddar cheese until melted. Add soda, cream and wine; mix well. Add seasonings. Simmer for 8 to 10 minutes, stirring frequently. Remove bay leaf. Ladle into heated bowls. Garnish with parsley or a sprinkle of paprika.

TOM'S EASY FISH CHOWDER

1/2 cup butter
2 tablespoons flour
1 pound boneless fish fillets, chopped
8 ounces bottled clam juice
2 6-ounce cans clams
1 lemon, sliced
1 16-ounce can white potatoes, drained
2 cups half and half
8 ounces peeled uncooked shrimp
12 mussels

Melt butter in large stockpot. Stir in flour until well mixed and mixture starts to bubble. Add fish, stirring to coat. Cook for 3 minutes or until fish is milky color. Add clam juice; mix well. Drain clams, reserving liquid. Chop clams. Add reserved clam liquid and lemon to fish mixture. Cook until mixture comes to a boil, stirring occasionally. Chop potatoes coarsely. Add to chowder. Bring to a boil. Add half and half and shrimp. Simmer until shrimp start to turn pink, stirring occasionally. Add chopped clams and mussels. Simmer for 5 minutes or until shrimp are pink and mussel shells have opened, stirring occasionally. Ladle into bowls. Serve with crackers.

Savory Lentil Soup

Yield:
6 servings
Utensil:
stockpot

Approx Per
Serving:
Cal 548
Prot 28 g
Carbo 49 g
Fiber 11 g
T Fat 28 g
Chol 66 mg
Sod 1051 mg

2 cups lentils
6 cups cold water
Salt to taste
3 stalks celery, sliced
1 medium onion, sliced
1   16-ounce can
    tomatoes

3 or 4 carrots, sliced
2 tablespoons bacon
    drippings
Pepper to taste
1   10-count package
    frankfurters, sliced

Wash lentils; drain. Combine lentils, water and salt in large stockpot. Simmer, covered, for 45 minutes, stirring occasionally. Add celery, onion, tomatoes, carrots, bacon drippings and pepper. Simmer for 30 minutes, stirring occasionally. Add frankfurter slices. Simmer for 30 minutes. Adjust seasoning.

Mrs. David's Macaroni Soup

Yield:
6 servings
Utensil:
saucepan

Approx Per
Serving:
Cal 70
Prot 2 g
Carbo 10 g
Fiber 1 g
T Fat 3 g
Chol 0 mg
Sod 123 mg

1   16-ounce can
    tomatoes
2 tomato cans water

Salt and pepper to taste
1 tablespoon oil
1/2 cup pastina

Combine tomatoes, water, salt and pepper in saucepan; mix well. Add oil. Simmer for 5 to 10 minutes. Add pastina. Simmer until tender-crisp, stirring frequently to prevent sticking. Remove from heat. Let soup stand for 10 minutes or until pastina is tender. Ladle into bowls.

Mrs. Potato Head Soup

<table>
<tr><td>

Yield:
10 servings
Utensil:
stockpot

---

*Approx Per
Serving:*
Cal 230
Prot 7 g
Carbo 39 g
Fiber 4 g
T Fat 6 g
Chol 19 mg
Sod 196 mg

</td></tr>
</table>

6 large potatoes, cubed
1 large onion, finely chopped
1 clove of garlic, minced
2 scallions, chopped
1/4 cup chopped fresh parsley
1 carrot, finely chopped
2 stalks celery, finely chopped
2 tablespoons butter
4 cups water
Salt and pepper to taste
4 cups milk
1 chicken bouillon cube
1/4 cup hot water
2 tablespoons flour

Combine potatoes, onion, garlic, scallions, parsley, carrot, celery, butter and water in stockpot. Simmer until vegetables are tender, stirring occasionally. Add salt, pepper and milk. Stir bouillon cube into hot water until dissolved. Stir in flour until well mixed. Add to soup; mix well. Simmer until soup is thickened, stirring frequently. Ladle into soup bowls. Garnish with parsley or dill.

Veal and Asparagus Easter Soup

<table>
<tr><td>

Yield:
12 servings
Utensil:
stockpot

---

*Approx Per
Serving:*
Cal 153
Prot 16 g
Carbo 4 g
Fiber 1 g
T Fat 8 g
Chol 85 mg
Sod 208 mg

</td></tr>
</table>

1 1/2 pounds stew veal
1/4 cup olive oil
2 onions, chopped
1 clove of garlic, minced
1 pound asparagus, coarsely chopped
1 16-ounce can chicken broth
Water
2 eggs
1/2 cup Romano cheese
Salt and pepper to taste

Sauté veal in olive oil in stockpot until brown. Add onions, garlic and asparagus. Cook for several minutes, stirring constantly. Add chicken broth and water to taste. Simmer until asparagus is tender, stirring frequently. Beat eggs with cheese until well mixed. Add a small amount of hot soup to eggs. Stir eggs into hot soup. Simmer for several minutes. Add salt and pepper. Ladle into soup bowls.

AMBROSIA SALAD

Yield:
12 servings
Utensil:
salad bowl

Approx Per Serving:
Cal 291
Prot 2 g
Carbo 50 g
Fiber 2 g
T Fat 10 g
Chol 17 mg
Sod 57 mg

1 16-ounce package colored miniature marshmallows
1 pint sour cream
1 16-ounce can crushed pineapple, drained
1 11-ounce can mandarin oranges, drained
1 8-ounce jar maraschino cherries, drained
1 3-ounce can coconut

Combine marshmallows, sour cream, pineapple, mandarin oranges, maraschino cherries and coconut in salad bowl; mix well. Chill in refrigerator until serving time.

CABBAGE SALAD

Yield:
12 servings
Utensil:
salad bowl

Approx Per Serving:
Cal 230
Prot 1 g
Carbo 28 g
Fiber 2 g
T Fat 14 g
Chol 0 mg
Sod 34 mg

6 cups shredded cabbage
2 medium carrots, shredded
1 small onion, finely chopped
1 green bell pepper, finely chopped
1 teaspoon celery seed
1/4 teaspoon mustard seed
3/4 cup oil
1/3 cup vinegar
1/3 cup water
1 cup sugar
1 3-ounce package lemon gelatin

Combine cabbage, carrots, onion, green pepper, celery seed and mustard seed in salad bowl; mix well. Combine oil, vinegar, water and sugar in saucepan; mix well. Bring to a boil. Stir in gelatin until dissolved. Pour over vegetables; mix well. Chill in refrigerator overnight.

CRISPY CABBAGE SALAD

Yield:
12 servings
Utensil:
salad bowl

**Approx Per
Serving:**
*Cal 125
Prot 1 g
Carbo 12 g
Fiber 1 g
T Fat 9 g
Chol 0 mg
Sod 142 mg*

1 head cabbage,
  shredded
1 large onion,
  shredded
2 carrots, shredded
1/2 cup vinegar

1/2 cup oil
1/3 cup honey
3/4 teaspoon dry
  mustard
3/4 teaspoon salt
1/2 teaspoon celery seed

Combine cabbage, onion and carrots in salad bowl; mix well. Combine vinegar, oil, honey, dry mustard, salt and celery seed in saucepan. Simmer for 2 minutes, stirring occasionally. Pour over cabbage mixture; mix well. Chill for 24 hours.

MARINATED CARROTS

Yield:
12 servings
Utensil:
salad bowl

**Approx Per
Serving:**
*Cal 202
Prot 1 g
Carbo 30 g
Fiber 3 g
T Fat 10 g
Chol 0 mg
Sod 196 mg*

2 pounds carrots,
  sliced
1 green bell pepper,
  chopped
1 red onion, chopped
1 10-ounce can
  tomato soup

1/4 to 1/2 cup oil
1 cup sugar
3/4 cup vinegar
1 teaspoon mustard
1 teaspoon
  Worcestershire sauce

Cook carrots in water in saucepan until tender-crisp; drain. Rinse in cold water; drain. Combine carrots, green pepper and onion in salad bowl; mix well. Combine tomato soup, oil, sugar, vinegar, mustard and Worcestershire sauce in saucepan. Bring to a boil. Pour over vegetables. Chill, covered, for 24 hours in refrigerator.

GREEN GELATIN SALAD

Yield:
15 servings
Utensil:
glass dish

Approx Per Serving:
Cal 285
Prot 5 g
Carbo 32 g
Fiber <1 g
T Fat 17 g
Chol 61 mg
Sod 139 mg

1 3-ounce package lemon gelatin
1 3-ounce package lime gelatin
2 cups boiling water
1¼ cups cold water
1 16-ounce can crushed pineapple
3 cups whipped topping
16 ounces cream cheese, softened
¾ cup sugar
2 tablespoons flour
2 eggs
¼ cup chopped pecans

Dissolve lemon and lime gelatin in boiling water in bowl. Add cold water; mix well. Drain pineapple, reserving 1 cup juice. Add pineapple to gelatin; mix well. Pour into 9x13-inch glass dish. Chill until set. Combine whipped topping and cream cheese in bowl; mix well. Spread over congealed gelatin. Chill in refrigerator. Combine reserved pineapple juice, sugar, flour and eggs in saucepan; mix well. Simmer until thickened, stirring constantly. Cool to room temperature. Pour over cream cheese layer. Sprinkle with pecans. Chill until serving time. Cut into squares.

CHEESE DILL MACARONI SALAD

Yield:
6 servings
Utensil:
salad bowl

Approx Per Serving:
Cal 432
Prot 13 g
Carbo 23 g
Fiber 1 g
T Fat 32 g
Chol 54 mg
Sod 383 mg

1½ cups uncooked macaroni
⅔ cup mayonnaise
4 teaspoons cider vinegar
1 teaspoon dill
2 cups cubed Cheddar cheese
⅔ cup sliced celery

Cook macaroni using package directions; drain. Cool to room temperature. Combine mayonnaise, cider vinegar and dill in salad bowl; mix well. Add cheese, celery and macaroni; toss to mix. Chill, covered, until serving time.

Hot German Potato Salad

Yield:
12 servings
Utensil:
salad bowl

Approx Per Serving:
Cal 268
Prot 8 g
Carbo 47 g
Fiber 5 g
T Fat 6 g
Chol 10 mg
Sod 373 mg

4 pounds potatoes
1 pound bacon
3 pounds onions, chopped
Salt and pepper to taste
1 teaspoon celery salt
3 tablespoons vinegar

Boil potatoes in water in saucepan until tender. Cool slightly at room temperature. Fry bacon in skillet until crisp. Drain bacon on paper towels. Reserve pan dripping in bowl. Sauté onions in 2 tablespoons reserved pan drippings in skillet. Peel potatoes; cut into slices. Combine potatoes, bacon, remaining pan drippings and onions in bowl; mix well. Add salt, pepper, celery salt and vinegar; mix well. Spoon into salad bowl. Serve hot.

Mom's Potato Salad

Yield:
6 servings
Utensil:
salad bowl

Approx Per Serving:
Cal 420
Prot 8 g
Carbo 55 g
Fiber 5 g
T Fat 20 g
Chol 122 mg
Sod 179 mg

2 to 2½ pounds boiled potatoes, cubed
½ cup chopped onion
½ cup chopped celery
½ cup mayonnaise
1 teaspoon prepared mustard
2 tablespoons sugar
¼ cup sour cream
Salt to taste
1 teaspoon parsley flakes
3 hard-boiled eggs, sliced

Combine potatoes, onion and celery in bowl; mix well. Combine mayonnaise, mustard and sugar in mixer bowl; beat well until sugar is dissolved. Add sour cream, salt and parsley flakes; mix well. Add dressing to salad; mix well. Spoon into salad bowl. Arrange egg slices around outer edge of salad bowl.

Pasta Lowell-Style

Yield:
6 servings
Utensil:
salad bowl

Approx Per
Serving:
Cal 365
Prot 16 g
Carbo 44 g
Fiber 5 g
T Fat 15 g
Chol 0 mg
Sod 522 mg

10 ounces uncooked bowtie pasta
1 large carrot, grated
1 medium cucumber, cubed
2/3 cup creamy peanut butter
3 tablespoons low-sodium soy sauce
1 14-ounce can low-salt chicken broth

Cook pasta using package directions until just tender. Rinse in cold water; drain. Combine pasta, carrot and cucumber in salad bowl; mix well. Combine peanut butter, soy sauce and chicken broth in saucepan. Simmer for 3 minutes or until well mixed, stirring frequently. Pour over pasta mixture; toss to mix. Chill in refrigerator for 1 hour to overnight. Mixture will look too moist but pasta will absorb most of liquid.

Beverly's Pasta Salad

Yield:
12 servings
Utensil:
large bowl

Approx Per
Serving:
Cal 444
Prot 15 g
Carbo 35 g
Fiber 3 g
T Fat 27 g
Chol 16 mg
Sod 945 mg

16 ounces tri-colored pasta
1 pound pepperoni
1 cup broccoli flowerets
1 red onion, chopped
1 carrot, finely chopped
1 cup sliced mushrooms
1 cup sliced celery
1 green bell pepper, chopped
1 envelope Good Seasons oil and vinegar salad dressing mix
Red wine vinegar
Olive oil
1 tablespoon honey
1 tablespoon Dijon mustard
1/2 cup Parmesan cheese
Salt and pepper to taste

Cook pasta using package directions; drain. Cool to room temperature. Cut pepperoni and broccoli into bite-sized pieces. Combine pasta, pepperoni, broccoli, onion, carrot, mushrooms, celery and green pepper in large bowl; mix well. Prepare salad dressing using package directions with red wine vinegar and olive oil in bowl. Add honey and mustard; mix well. Add dressing to salad; mix well. Add Parmesan cheese, salt and pepper; mix well. Chill until serving time.

Spinach Salad with Pine Nuts

Yield:
8 servings
Utensil:
salad bowl

Approx Per Serving:
Cal 187
Prot 6 g
Carbo 3 g
Fiber 1 g
T Fat 18 g
Chol 89 mg
Sod 260 mg

2 bunches fresh spinach
1 teaspoon soda
2 tablespoons oil
1 tablepsoon lemon juice
Special Spinach Salad Dressing

3 hard-boiled eggs, chopped
1/2 cup chopped pine nuts
4 slices crisp-fried bacon, crumbled

Wash spinach in mixture of cold water and soda; rinse. Tear into 1-inch pieces, discarding stems. Combine with 2 tablespoons oil and lemon juice in salad bowl. Chill until serving time. Pour Special Spinach Salad Dressing over spinach. Sprinkle with chopped eggs, pine nuts and bacon. Garnish with sliced tomatoes and asparagus.

Special Spinach Salad Dressing

Yield:
8 servings
Utensil:
mixer bowl

Approx Per Serving:
Cal 529
Prot 2 g
Carbo 7 g
Fiber <1 g
T Fat 56 g
Chol 53 mg
Sod 468 mg

1 clove of garlic, split
2 eggs
1 tablespoon sugar
1 teaspoon salt
1/2 teaspoon paprika
1/2 teaspoon dry mustard

1 teaspoon Worcestershire sauce
1/2 cup catsup
2 cups oil
1/2 cup vinegar
2/3 cup warm water

Rub mixer bowl with garlic. Add eggs, sugar, salt, paprika, dry mustard, Worcestershire sauce and catsup; mix well. Add oil alternately with vinegar, mixing well after addition. Add warm water gradually, mixing until smooth and of desired consistency.

SINFUL STRAWBERRY SALAD

Yield:
12 servings
Utensil:
glass dish

Approx Per Serving:
Cal 268
Prot 4 g
Carbo 33 g
Fiber 3 g
T Fat 15 g
Chol 17 mg
Sod 67 mg

1 6-ounce package strawberry gelatin
1 cup boiling water
2 10-ounce packages frozen strawberries, thawed, drained
1 20-ounce can crushed pineapple, drained
3 bananas, mashed
1 cup chopped pecans
1 pint sour cream

Dissolve gelatin in boiling water in bowl. Add strawberries and pineapple; mix well. Stir in bananas and pecans. Pour half the mixture into 8x12-inch glass dish. Chill until set. Let remaining gelatin mixture stand at room temperature. Spread sour cream over congealed mixture. Spoon remaining gelatin mixture onto sour cream. Chill until set or overnight.

TUNA-APPLE SALAD

Yield:
4 servings
Utensil:
salad plates

Approx Per Serving:
Cul 237
Prot 14 g
Carbo 31 g
Fiber 3 g
T Fat 8 g
Chol 32 mg
Sod 307 mg

1 cup finely chopped green bell pepper
2 cups unpeeled chopped apples
1 6-ounce can water-pack tuna, drained
2 teaspoons sesame seed, toasted
1/2 cup raisins
1/2 cup low-fat mayonnaise
4 lettuce leaves

Combine green pepper, apple, tuna, sesame seed, raisins and mayonnaise in bowl; mix well. Spoon onto lettuce-lined salad plates.

CAESAR DRESSING

Yield:
60 servings
Utensil:
container

4 cups olive oil
¼ cup Worcestershire
  sauce
6 cloves of garlic,
  minced

Juice of 6 lemons
4 teaspoons Dijon
  mustard
Freshly ground pepper
  to taste

**Approx Per
Serving:**
*Cal 130
Prot <1 g
Carbo 1 g
Fiber <1 g
T Fat 14 g
Chol 0 mg
Sod 14 mg*

Combine olive oil, Worcestershire sauce, garlic, lemon juice, mustard and pepper in container; mix well. Store, covered, in refrigerator. Mix well before serving over mixed greens.

RASPBERRY VINAIGRETTE SALAD DRESSING

Yield:
3 quarts
Utensil:
container

2 eggs
2 quarts vegetable oil
2 cups red wine
  vinegar
1 cup sugar
2 cups Melba sauce
1½ teaspoons basil

1½ teaspoons thyme
1½ teaspoons oregano
1½ teaspoons tarragon
Salt and pepper to
  taste
Garlic powder to taste

*Nutritional
information for
this recipe is
not available.*

Beat eggs in mixer bowl until frothy. Add oil slowly, beating to form a temporary emulsion. Add vinegar; beat for 15 seconds. Add sugar, Melba sauce, basil, thyme, oregano, tarragon, salt, pepper and garlic powder; beat well. Store in covered container in refrigerator. Shake or mix vigorously before serving. Melba sauce is a raspberry sauce available at specialty food stores.

MEATS

New England Lighthouse

Biaciole

Yield:
6 servings
Utensil:
skillet

Approx Per
Serving:
Cal 219
Prot 23 g
Carbo 6 g
Fiber 1 g
T Fat 11 g
Chol 64 mg
Sod 544 mg

1 1½-pound flank
   steak
2 tablespoons olive oil
2 cloves of garlic,
   minced
1 tablespoon grated
   Parmesan cheese

1 teaspoon each
   pepper, oregano,
   basil and tarragon
2 cups tomato sauce

Spread steak with olive oil and garlic. Sprinkle cheese, pepper, oregano, basil and tarragon on steak. Roll to enclose seasonings; secure with string. Combine with tomato sauce in skillet small enough that sauce covers steak completely. Simmer for several hours or until done to taste.

Chimichangas

Yield:
4 servings
Utensil:
baking dish

Approx Per
Serving:
Cal 556
Prot 34 g
Carbo 36 g
Fiber 2 g
T Fat 31 g
Chol 94 mg
Sod 748 mg

2½ cups shredded
   cooked beef
⅔ cup picante sauce
⅓ cup onion slices
¾ to 1 teaspoon cumin
½ teaspoon oregano

8 7 to 8-inch flour
   tortillas
¼ cup melted
   margarine
1 cup shredded
   Monterey Jack cheese

Combine beef, picante sauce, onion, cumin and oregano in saucepan. Simmer for 5 minutes or until most of the liquid is absorbed. Brush 1 side of tortillas with melted margarine. Spoon beef mixture onto center of unbuttered sides of tortillas; top with cheese. Fold 2 sides over filling; fold ends down. Place seam side down in 9x13-inch baking dish. Bake at 475 degrees for 13 to 15 minutes or until crisp and golden brown.

Hungarian Goulash

Yield:
4 servings
Utensil:
skillet

Approx Per
Serving:
Cal 356
Prot 30 g
Carbo 26 g
Fiber 2 g
T Fat 15 g
Chol 100 mg
Sod 573 mg

1¹/₃ pounds round
  steak
2 tablespoons butter
2 large Bermuda
  onions, chopped
¹/₄ teaspoon dry
  mustard
1 teaspoon paprika
2 tablespoons
  Worcestershire sauce

2 tablespoons brown
  sugar
6 tablespoons catsup
1 cup water
¹/₂ teaspoon cider
  vinegar
¹/₄ teaspoon salt
3 tablespoons
  cornstarch
¹/₂ cup water

Trim round steak; cut into 1-inch cubes. Brown on all sides in butter in skillet. Remove with slotted spoon. Sauté onions in pan drippings in skillet until tender. Stir in beef. Combine dry mustard, paprika, Worcestershire sauce, brown sugar, catsup, 1 cup water, vinegar and salt in bowl; mix well. Pour over beef. Simmer, covered, at medium-low heat for 2¹/₂ hours. Blend cornstarch and ¹/₂ cup water in bowl. Stir into skillet. Cook until thickened, stirring frequently. Serve over wide egg noodles.

Deviled Short Ribs

Yield:
4 servings
Utensil:
saucepan

Approx Per
Serving:
Cal 1050
Prot 104 g
Carbo 38 g
Fiber 3 g
T Fat 52 g
Chol 299 mg
Sod 1218 mg

4 to 5 pounds beef
  short ribs
1 15-ounce can
  tomato sauce
1 6-ounce can frozen
  lemonade
  concentrate
1 medium onion,
  sliced into rings
¹/₄ cup chopped fresh
  parsley

2 tablespoons brown
  sugar
2 teaspoons
  Worcestershire sauce
¹/₂ teaspoon thyme
1 bay leaf
¹/₂ teaspoon celery salt
¹/₂ teaspoon crushed
  red pepper

Combine short ribs with tomato sauce, lemonade concentrate, onion, parsley, brown sugar, Worcestershire sauce, thyme, bay leaf, celery salt and red pepper in heavy saucepan. Bring to a boil; reduce heat. Simmer, covered, for 2¹/₂ to 3 hours or until ribs are fork-tender. Skim fat from surface of sauce; discard bay leaf.

Cajun Roast

Yield:
8 servings
Utensil:
baking pan

Approx Per Serving:
Cal 308
Prot 43 g
Carbo 2 g
Fiber 1 g
T Fat 13 g
Chol 128 mg
Sod 195 mg

1 4-pound beef roast
6 cloves of garlic
3 jalapeño peppers
1 bunch scallions
Salt, pepper and cayenne pepper to taste

Cut slits in roast. Press garlic, peppers and scallions into slits. Sprinkle with salt, pepper and cayenne pepper. Place in baking pan. Bake at 325 degrees for 20 minutes per pound or until done to taste. May place on spit and grill until done to taste if preferred. Serve with seasoned potatoes grilled in foil. May substitute bell pepper strips for jalapeño peppers if desired.

Chinese Pot Roast

Yield:
8 servings
Utensil:
skillet

Approx Per Serving:
Cal 346
Prot 44 g
Carbo 4 g
Fiber 1 g
T Fat 16 g
Chol 128 mg
Sod 585 mg

1 4-pound chuck roast
2 tablespoons shortening
1/4 cup water
1/4 cup soy sauce
1/2 teaspoon ginger
1 clove of garlic, minced
2 medium onions, sliced

Brown roast on all sides in shortening in heavy skillet. Combine water, soy sauce, ginger, garlic and onions in bowl; mix well. Add to skillet. Simmer, covered, for 2 1/2 hours or until tender.

SUPER-EASY POT ROAST

Yield:
8 servings
Utensil:
baking dish

Approx Per Serving:
Cal 342
Prot 43 g
Carbo 10 g
Fiber 1 g
T Fat 13 g
Chol 128 mg
Sod 427 mg

1 4-pound boneless chuck roast

²/₃ cup ginger ale
1 cup catsup

Place roast in baking dish. Combine ginger ale and catsup in bowl; mix well. Pour over roast; cover with lid or foil. Bake at 325 degrees for 3 to 4 hours or until done to taste.

SAVORY POT ROAST

Yield:
8 servings
Utensil:
saucepan

Approx Per Serving:
Cal 406
Prot 44 g
Carbo 11 g
Fiber 2 g
T Fat 19 g
Chol 144 mg
Sod 368 mg

1 4-pound pot roast
2 tablespoons flour
¹/₂ teaspoon salt
¹/₄ teaspoon pepper
¹/₄ cup butter
3 onions, sliced

3 carrots, sliced
2 stalks celery, sliced
¹/₂ cup tomato sauce
2 cups water
1 bay leaf
¹/₂ cup red wine

Wipe roast with damp cloth; sprinkle with flour, salt and pepper, coating well. Brown on all sides in butter in heavy saucepan. Add onions. Sauté until onions are tender. Add carrots, celery, tomato sauce, water, bay leaf and wine. Simmer, covered, for 3 hours. Slice roast. Serve with sauce, discarding bay leaf. Serve with potatoes if desired.

STEAK TIPS

Yield:
6 servings
Utensil:
baking pan

Approx Per
Serving:
Cal 552
Prot 29 g
Carbo 8 g
Fiber <1 g
T Fat 54 g
Chol 85 mg
Sod 416 mg

2 pounds beef   1   16-ounce bottle of
    tenderloin   Italian salad dressing

Cut beef into bite-sized pieces. Combine with salad
dressing in airtight container. Marinate overnight,
stirring several times; drain. Thread beef onto
skewers; place in baking pan. Bake at 350 degrees
for 10 minutes. Serve with rice pilaf and salad.

*Nutritional information includes entire amount of
marinade.*

MARINADE FOR BEEF TIPS

Yield:
8 servings
Utensil:
bowl

Approx Per
Serving:
Cal 137
Prot <1 g
Carbo 2 g
Fiber <1 g
T Fat 14 g
Chol 0 mg
Sod 171 mg

¹/₂ cup oil   1 tablespoon vinegar
¹/₂ cup red wine   ¹/₂ teaspoon marjoram
2 tablespoons   1 clove of garlic,
    Worcestershire sauce   minced
1 teaspoon sugar   ¹/₂ teaspoon salt

Combine oil, wine, Worcestershire sauce, sugar,
vinegar, marjoram, garlic and salt in bowl; mix well.
Use to marinate beef tips. May also use to marinate
vegetables or other meat for shish kabobs.

CORNED BEEF DINNER

Yield:
6 servings
Utensil:
saucepan

Approx Per Serving:
Cal 623
Prot 50 g
Carbo 77 g
Fiber 11 g
T Fat 14 g
Chol 128 mg
Sod 141 mg

1 3-pound corned beef brisket
1/2 cup chopped onion
1/4 cup packed brown sugar
2 cloves of garlic, minced
1 teaspoon dry mustard
Cloves to taste
2 bay leaves
6 medium potatoes, cut into halves
6 carrots, cut into halves
2 pounds cabbage, cut into 6 wedges

Combine brisket with water to cover in heavy saucepan. Add onion, brown sugar, garlic, dry mustard, cloves and bay leaves. Bring to a boil; reduce heat. Simmer, covered, for 3 to 3½ hours or until brisket is fork-tender. Add potatoes and carrots. Simmer for 30 minutes. Remove brisket to serving platter. Add cabbage to saucepan. Simmer, covered, for 20 to 25 minutes or until cabbage is tender. Cut brisket into ¼-inch slices. Arrange vegetables around beef, discarding bay leaves.

CORNED BEEF VON REUBEN

Yield:
8 servings
Utensil:
baking dish

Approx Per Serving:
Cal 406
Prot 29 g
Carbo 27 g
Fiber 1 g
T Fat 20 g
Chol 177 mg
Sod 1314 mg

1 8-ounce package seasoned croutons
1 12-ounce can corned beef, crumbled
1 16-ounce can sauerkraut, drained
8 ounces Swiss cheese, sliced
4 eggs
2 cups milk

Sprinkle half the croutons in buttered 8x11-inch baking dish. Layer corned beef, sauerkraut, remaining croutons and cheese in prepared dish. Beat eggs with milk in bowl. Pour over layers. Bake at 325 to 350 degrees for 35 minutes or until brown.

CHILI

Yield:
8 servings
Utensil:
saucepan

Approx Per
Serving:
Cal 400
Prot 28 g
Carbo 37 g
Fiber 13 g
T Fat 17 g
Chol 56 mg
Sod 749 mg

1½ pounds ground beef
1 large onion, chopped
2 medium stalks celery, sliced
4 cloves of garlic, crushed
1 large green bell pepper, sliced
2 tablespoons olive oil
1 16-ounce can whole tomatoes

1 6-ounce can tomato paste
2 to 3 tablespoons chili powder
1 tablespoon Worcestershire sauce
½ teaspoon pepper sauce
2 teaspoons salt
Pepper to taste
2 16-ounce cans kidney beans, drained

Brown ground beef with onion, celery, garlic and green pepper in olive oil in 3-quart saucepan, stirring frequently; drain. Stir in undrained tomatoes, tomato paste, chili powder, Worcestershire sauce, pepper sauce, salt and pepper. Bring to a boil; reduce heat. Simmer, covered, for 1 hour. Add beans. Simmer for 15 minutes or until chili is of desired consistency.

HAMBURGER CHOP SUEY

Yield:
6 servings
Utensil:
skillet

Approx Per
Serving:
Cal 430
Prot 22 g
Carbo 48 g
Fiber 5 g
T Fat 17 g
Chol 50 mg
Sod 1163 mg

½ cup slivered almonds
1 pound ground beef
1 medium onion, sliced
2 large stalks celery, sliced
1 tablespoon instant beef bouillon
2 cups hot water
¼ cup cold water
3 tablespoons soy sauce

2 tablespoons cornstarch
¼ teaspoon MSG
1 16-ounce can bean sprouts, drained
1 8-ounce can sliced water chestnuts, drained
4 cups hot cooked rice
1 2-ounce jar sliced pimento, drained

Sprinkle almonds on baking sheet. Toast in 350-degree oven for 10 to 15 minutes or until golden brown, stirring occasionally. Brown ground beef in 10-inch skillet over medium heat, stirring until crumbly; drain. Stir in onion, celery, bouillon and hot water. Bring to a boil; reduce heat. Combine cold water, soy sauce, cornstarch and MSG in covered container; shake until smooth. Add to ground beef mixture. Cook for 1 minute or until thickened, stirring constantly. Add bean sprouts and water chestnuts. Cook until heated through. Serve over rice. Top with almonds and pimento.

Stuffed Eggplant

Yield:
4 servings
Utensil:
baking pan

Approx Per
Serving:
Cal 329
Prot 26 g
Carbo 14 g
Fiber 5 g
T Fat 19 g
Chol 85 mg
Sod 466 mg

1 large eggplant
1 pound ground beef
1 small onion, chopped
1 green bell pepper,
  chopped
1 cup chopped
  mushrooms
1/2 teaspoon oregano
1/2 teaspoon basil
Chopped parsley, salt
  and pepper to taste
1 8-ounce can tomato
  sauce
1/2 cup shredded
  mozzarella cheese

Cut eggplant into halves lengthwise. Remove and chop pulp, reserving 1/2-inch shells. Combine shells with hot water to cover in bowl; let stand while preparing filling. Brown ground beef in skillet, stirring until crumbly; drain. Add chopped eggplant pulp, onion, green pepper, mushrooms, oregano, basil, parsley, salt and pepper; mix well. Cook until vegetables are tender-crisp. Drain eggplant shells well. Spoon filling into shells; place in baking pan. Pour tomato sauce over top; sprinkle with cheese. Bake at 350 degrees for 30 minutes.

Hamburgers Polynesian

Yield:
4 servings
Utensil:
grill

Approx Per
Serving:
Cal 426
Prot 23 g
Carbo 48 g
Fiber 1 g
T Fat 17 g
Chol 74 mg
Sod 629 mg

1 pound ground beef
4 pineapple rings
1/2 cup catsup
1/2 cup packed brown
  sugar
1/4 cup mustard

Shape ground beef into 8 patties. Place 1 pineapple ring on half the patties; top with remaining patties, pressing edges to enclose pineapple. Combine catsup, brown sugar and mustard in saucepan. Heat to serving temperature, stirring to mix well. Grill or broil hamburger patties until done to taste. Serve with sauce.

Lazy Lasagna

Yield:
4 servings
Utensil:
baking dish

Approx Per Serving:
Cal 842
Prot 46 g
Carbo 72 g
Fiber 2 g
T Fat 42 g
Chol 124 mg
Sod 1253 mg

8 ounces uncooked wide egg noodles
1 cup ricotta cheese
2/3 cup shredded mozzarella cheese
1/3 cup grated Parmesan cheese
1 pound ground beef
3 cups spaghetti sauce

Cook noodles using package directions; drain. Combine with ricotta cheese, mozzarella cheese and Parmesan cheese in bowl; toss to mix well. Brown ground beef in skillet, stirring until crumbly; drain. Add spaghetti sauce; mix well. Spread thin layer of meat sauce in shallow 2-quart baking dish. Layer noodle mixture and remaining meat sauce 1/2 at a time in prepared dish. Bake at 375 degrees for 25 to 30 minutes or until bubbly.

Sweet and Sour Meatballs

Yield:
6 servings
Utensil:
skillet

Approx Per Serving:
Cal 404
Prot 24 g
Carbo 39 g
Fiber 1 g
T Fat 18 g
Chol 110 mg
Sod 694 mg

1 1/2 pounds ground beef
2/3 cup bread crumbs
1/3 cup minced onion
1 egg
1/2 teaspoon ginger
1 teaspoon salt
1/2 cup water
2 tablespoons cornstarch
1/2 cup packed brown sugar
1/3 cup vinegar
1 tablespoon soy sauce
1/2 cup chopped green bell pepper
1 13-ounce can pineapple tidbits, drained

Combine ground beef, bread crumbs, onion, egg, ginger and salt in bowl; mix well. Shape into 2-inch meatballs. Brown on all sides in skillet; drain. Add water. Simmer, covered, for 2 to 3 minutes. Blend cornstarch, brown sugar, vinegar and soy sauce in small saucepan. Cook until thickened, stirring constantly. Cook for 1 minute longer, stirring constantly. Add green pepper and pineapple. Pour over meatballs. Heat to serving temperature.

MEATBALLS

Yield:
4 servings
Utensil:
skillet

Approx Per
Serving:
Cal 314
Prot 27 g
Carbo 7 g
Fiber <1 g
T Fat 20 g
Chol 133 mg
Sod 268 mg

1 pound ground beef
1 egg
1/3 cup bread crumbs
1 clove of garlic,
   minced

1/3 cup grated
   Parmesan cheese
2 tablespoons chopped
   parsley
1/4 cup cold water

Combine ground beef, egg, bread crumbs, garlic, cheese, parsley and water in bowl; mix well. Shape into meatballs. Brown on all sides in skillet.

DUTCH MEAT LOAF

Yield:
6 servings
Utensil:
loaf pan

Approx Per
Serving:
Cal 338
Prot 25 g
Carbo 19 g
Fiber 2 g
T Fat 18 g
Chol 110 mg
Sod 997 mg

1 1/2 pounds ground
   beef
1 cup fresh bread
   crumbs
1 medium onion,
   chopped
1 egg
1 1/2 teaspoons salt

1/4 teaspoon pepper
1 8-ounce can tomato
   sauce
1/2 cup water
1 tablespoon mustard
1 tablespoon vinegar
1 tablespoon molasses

Combine ground beef, bread crumbs, onion, egg, salt and pepper in bowl; mix well. Press into loaf pan. Combine tomato sauce, water, mustard, vinegar and molasses in small bowl; mix well. Pour over meat loaf. Bake at 350 degrees for 1 hour and 15 minutes.

ITALIAN MEAT LOAF

Yield:
6 servings
Utensil:
loaf pan

Approx Per
Serving:
Cal 340
Prot 26 g
Carbo 16 g
Fiber 1 g
T Fat 19 g
Chol 113 mg
Sod 846 mg

1¹/₂ pounds lean
   ground beef
1 8-ounce can tomato
   sauce
1 egg
1 cup Italian-style
   bread crumbs
¹/₂ cup chopped onion
¹/₄ cup grated
   Parmesan cheese
¹/₈ teaspoon garlic
   powder
1 teaspoon salt
¹/₄ teaspoon pepper

Combine ground beef, tomato sauce, egg, bread
crumbs, onion, cheese, garlic powder, salt and pepper in bowl; mix well. Shape into loaf in loaf pan.
Bake at 350 degrees for 40 minutes.

ANOTHER ITALIAN MEAT LOAF

Yield:
6 servings
Utensil:
loaf pan

Approx Per
Serving:
Cal 255
Prot 18 g
Carbo 7 g
Fiber 1 g
T Fat 17 g
Chol 94 mg
Sod 277 mg

1 pound ground beef
6 ounces hot Italian
   sausage
1 14-ounce can
   stewed tomatoes
1 cup bread crumbs
¹/₂ cup chopped onion
¹/₂ cup chopped green
   bell pepper
1 egg, beaten

Combine ground beef, sausage, tomatoes, bread
crumbs, onion, green pepper and egg in bowl; mix
well. Place in 4x8-inch loaf pan. Bake at 350 degrees
for 1 hour; drain before serving. May use spicy bulk
sausage if preferred.

MEAT LOAF

<table>
<tr><td>

Yield:
8 servings
Utensil:
loaf pan

</td></tr>
<tr><td>

Approx Per
Serving:
Cal 327
Prot 16 g
Carbo 10 g
Fiber 1 g
T Fat 25 g
Chol 97 mg
Sod 234 mg

</td></tr>
</table>

1 pound lean ground beef
2 eggs
1/2 cup bread crumbs
1/2 cup oats
1/4 cup bran
1/2 cup grated Romano cheese
1/2 cup olive oil
Onion powder and garlic powder to taste
1/4 teaspoon salt
1/4 teaspoon pepper

Combine ground beef, eggs, bread crumbs, oats, bran, cheese, olive oil, onion powder, garlic powder, salt and pepper in bowl; mix well. Place in loaf pan. Bake at 350 degrees for 30 to 40 minutes or until done to taste.

TACO CASSEROLE

<table>
<tr><td>

Yield:
6 servings
Utensil:
baking dish

</td></tr>
<tr><td>

Approx Per
Serving:
Cal 599
Prot 32 g
Carbo 44 g
Fiber 9 g
T Fat 33 g
Chol 90 mg
Sod 1556 mg

</td></tr>
</table>

1 pound ground beef
3/4 cup chopped onion
1 envelope taco seasoning mix
3/4 cup water
1 16-ounce can refried beans
1 8-ounce jar taco sauce
1 7-ounce package tortilla chips, crushed
2 cups shredded Cheddar cheese

Brown ground beef with onion in medium skillet, stirring frequently; drain. Add taco seasoning mix and water. Simmer for 20 minutes. Combine beans and taco sauce in medium bowl; mix well. Reserve half the chips and cheese. Layer half the bean mixture, half the meat sauce, remaining chips and remaining cheese in 8x8-inch baking dish. Top with remaining bean mixture and meat sauce. Bake at 400 degrees for 25 minutes. Sprinkle with reserved chips and cheese. Bake until cheese melts.

ZITI BAKE

Yield:
8 servings
Utensil:
baking dish

Approx Per Serving:
Cal 642
Prot 34 g
Carbo 62 g
Fiber 4 g
T Fat 29 g
Chol 116 mg
Sod 998 mg

1 16-ounce package ziti
1 pound ground beef
15 ounces ricotta cheese
1/2 cup grated Parmesan cheese
1/4 cup chopped fresh parsley
1 egg, slightly beaten
3/4 teaspoon salt
1/4 teaspoon pepper
1 29-ounce jar spaghetti sauce
8 ounces mozzarella cheese, shredded

Cook pasta using package directions; drain. Brown ground beef in heavy saucepan for 10 minutes, stirring until crumbly. Remove from heat and drain. Stir in ricotta cheese, Parmesan cheese, parsley, egg, salt, pepper and half the spaghetti sauce; mix well. Add ziti; toss gently to mix. Spoon into 9x13-inch baking dish. Spread remaining spaghetti sauce over top; sprinkle with mozzarella cheese. Bake at 350 degrees for 30 minutes or until bubbly.

CHINESE PORK STRIPS

Yield:
8 servings
Utensil:
baking dish

Approx Per Serving:
Cal 313
Prot 24 g
Carbo 37 g
Fiber <1 g
T Fat 8 g
Chol 72 mg
Sod 462 mg

2 pounds fresh pork shoulder
4 teaspoons honey
4 teaspoons sugar
1 tablespoon soy sauce
4 drops of red food coloring (optional)
1/3 cup hot water
1 teaspoon salt
1 12-ounce jar plum jelly
6 ounces finely chopped chutney
4 teaspoons sugar
5 teaspoons vinegar

Cut pork into several long strips. Combine with honey, 4 teaspoons sugar, soy sauce, food coloring, water and salt in baking dish; mix well. Marinate in refrigerator for 4 hours, turning pork several times. Bake at 350 degrees for 1 1/2 hours, basting occasionally. Combine plum jelly, chutney, 4 teaspoons sugar and vinegar in bowl; mix well. Slice pork; serve with plum sauce. May substitute stock for water if preferred.

Nutritional information does not include chutney.

TERIYAKI PINEAPPLE PORK CHOPS

Yield:
4 servings
Utensil:
grill

Approx Per
Serving:
Cal 333
Prot 33 g
Carbo 26 g
Fiber 1 g
T Fat 11 g
Chol 98 mg
Sod 1113 mg

1 8-ounce can
pineapple slices
1/4 cup packed brown
sugar
1/4 cup soy sauce

1/4 teaspoon garlic
powder
4 1-inch center-cut
pork chops

Drain pineapple, reserving juice. Combine with brown sugar, soy sauce and garlic powder in 8x12-inch baking dish; mix well. Add pork chops, turning to coat well. Marinate, covered, for 6 to 8 hours, turning chops once. Drain, reserving marinade. Grill pork chops until tender, basting frequently with reserved marinade. Place pineapple slices on grill. Grill for 8 minutes or until heated through, turning once and brushing with marinade. Serve pineapple on pork chops.

SWEET AND SOUR PORK CHOPS

Yield:
4 servings
Utensil:
baking pan

Approx Per
Serving:
Cal 310
Prot 32 g
Carbo 21 g
Fiber 1 g
T Fat 11 g
Chol 98 mg
Sod 86 mg

4 medium pork chops
1/3 cup packed brown
sugar
1 tablespoon cider or
white vinegar
1 teaspoon sage
1 teaspoon paprika

1 teaspoon dry mustard
1/2 teaspoon garlic
powder
1/4 teaspoon freshly
ground pepper
1 medium onion, sliced

Trim chops; arrange in teflon-coated baking pan. Combine brown sugar, vinegar, sage, paprika, dry mustard, garlic powder and pepper in bowl; mix well. Spread over pork chops; top with onion slices. Bake at 350 degrees for 1 hour. Serve with baked potatoes and winter squash.

Roast Pork Loin

Yield:
8 servings
Utensil:
roasting pan

Approx Per Serving:
Cal 441
Prot 49 g
Carbo 24 g
Fiber 1 g
T Fat 15 g
Chol 140 mg
Sod 644 mg

1 4-pound pork loin
2 teaspoons rosemary
2 teaspoons thyme
2 cups flour
4 teaspoons garlic powder
2 teaspoons salt
2 teaspoons pepper

Trim pork loin. Rub with rosemary and thyme. Mix flour, garlic powder, salt and pepper together. Coat pork with mixture. Place in roasting pan. Place in preheated 450-degree oven; reduce temperature to 325 degrees. Roast for 30 minutes per pound.

Easy Sausage Bake

Yield:
6 servings
Utensil:
baking dish

Approx Per Serving:
Cal 428
Prot 9 g
Carbo 30 g
Fiber 3 g
T Fat 31 g
Chol 36 mg
Sod 533 mg

1¹/2 pounds link sausages, cut into halves
3 large potatoes, cut into 1-inch pieces
2 green bell peppers, cut into 1-inch pieces
1 large onion, coarsely chopped
¹/4 cup olive oil
¹/2 teaspoon basil
¹/2 teaspoon oregano
¹/2 teaspoon garlic salt
¹/4 teaspoon pepper

Combine sausages, potatoes, green peppers, onion, olive oil, basil, oregano, garlic salt and pepper in bowl; mix well. Spoon into 9x13-inch baking dish. Bake at 350 degrees for 1 hour or until brown, stirring every 15 minutes.

KIELBASA

1 pound kielbasa
1 medium-large onion, chopped
4 cloves of garlic, chopped
¼ cup olive oil
¼ teaspoon pepper

Cook kielbasa in water in saucepan for 20 minutes; drain. Cool and slice. Sauté onion and garlic in olive oil in saucepan until transparent. Add kielbasa and pepper. Simmer for 5 to 10 minutes or until heated through. Drain to serve.

ITALIAN CASSEROLE

6 Italian sausages
1 large onion, chopped
1 small eggplant, unpeeled, chopped
2 small zucchini, unpeeled, chopped
2 4-ounce cans sliced mushrooms, drained
3 large green bell peppers, chopped
¼ cup olive oil
½ cup spaghetti sauce
¼ cup grated Romano cheese

Pierce skins of sausages with fork; place in baking dish. Spread onion, eggplant, zucchini and mushrooms over sausages. Top with green peppers. Drizzle with olive oil. Bake at 375 degrees for 35 to 40 minutes or until sausages are cooked through and vegetables are tender. Remove and slice sausages. Return to baking dish. Pour spaghetti sauce over top; sprinkle with cheese. Bake until heated through.

Sausage Macaroni and Cheese

Yield:
6 servings
Utensil:
baking dish

Approx Per
Serving:
Cal 564
Prot 21 g
Carbo 51 g
Fiber 3 g
T Fat 31 g
Chol 62 mg
Sod 1187 mg

1 pound hot or mild
 Italian sausages
11 to 12 ounces
 uncooked
 macaroni
1 onion, chopped

8 ounces American
 cheese, cut into
 1/2-inch cubes
1 10-ounce can cream
 of mushroom soup
4 crackers, crushed

Place sausages in baking dish. Bake at 400 degrees for 30 to 35 minutes. Drain and slice sausages. Cook macaroni using package directions. Combine with onion, cheese and sausages in bowl; mix well. Add soup; toss with 2 forks to mix well. Spoon into 2½-quart baking dish sprayed with nonstick cooking spray. Top with cracker crumbs. Bake at 350 degrees for 30 minutes. May use Monterey Jack cheese, with or without jalapeño peppers, or hot pepper American cheese if preferred.

Venison Goulash

Yield:
6 servings
Utensil:
skillet

Approx Per
Serving:
Cal 238
Prot 29 g
Carbo 16 g
Fiber 1 g
T Fat 6 g
Chol 61 mg
Sod 516 mg

2 pounds 1-inch
 venison cubes
1 onion, sliced
1/8 teaspoon garlic
 powder
2 tablespoons
 margarine
1½ cups water
3/4 cup catsup
2 tablespoons
 Worcestershire sauce

1 tablespoon brown
 sugar
2 teaspoons paprika
1/2 teaspoon dry
 mustard
Pepper sauce to taste
1/4 cup cold water
2 tablespoons flour

Brown venison with onion and garlic powder in margarine in 2-inch deep skillet. Stir in 1½ cups water, catsup, Worcestershire sauce, brown sugar, paprika, dry mustard and pepper sauce. Bring to a boil; reduce heat. Simmer, covered, for 2 to 2½ hours or until venison is tender. Combine 1/4 cup water and flour in covered container; shake to mix well. Stir into goulash. Cook until thickened, stirring constantly. Cook for 1 minute, stirring constantly. Serve over egg noodles.

POULTRY

Rockport Harbor
Rockport, Massachusetts

Chicken Bake

Yield:
4 servings
Utensil:
baking dish

Approx Per Serving:
Cal 390
Prot 23 g
Carbo 20 g
Fiber 1 g
T Fat 24 g
Chol 67 mg
Sod 395 mg

4 chicken breast filets
1/2 cup mayonnaise
1 tablespoon garlic
   paste
Pepper to taste
1 cup bread crumbs

Rinse chicken and pat dry. Combine mayonnaise and garlic paste in bowl; mix well. Spread on both sides of chicken; sprinkle with pepper. Coat with bread crumbs. Arrange in oiled baking dish. Bake at 350 degrees for 20 to 22 minutes or until tender.

Barbecued Chicken

Yield:
5 servings
Utensil:
2 brown bags

Approx Per Serving:
Cal 278
Prot 40 g
Carbo 1 g
Fiber <1 g
T Fat 12 g
Chol 126 mg
Sod 186 mg

1 chicken, cut-up
Salt to taste
2 teaspoons vinegar
2 teaspoons
   Worcestershire sauce
4 teaspoons water
1 teaspoon prepared
   mustard
2 teaspoons catsup
2 teaspoons melted
   butter
2 teaspoons lemon
   juice
1 teaspoon chili
   powder
1 teaspoon paprika
1/4 teaspoon red pepper

Select 2 brown paper bags made of nonrecycled material: recycled material may release dangerous elements when heated. Place 1 bag inside the other; grease the inside of the inner bag. Rinse chicken and pat dry; sprinkle with salt. Combine vinegar, Worcestershire sauce, water, mustard, catsup, butter, lemon juice, chili powder, paprika and red pepper in bowl; mix well. Dip chicken in sauce, coating well. Place chicken in bags. Secure opening of bags; place on baking sheet. Bake at 325 degrees for 2 hours.

Chicken Chow Mein

Yield:
10 servings
Utensil:
baking dish

*Approx Per
Serving:*
Cal 442
Prot 44 g
Carbo 16 g
Fiber 2 g
T Fat 22 g
Chol 124 mg
Sod 1053 mg

2 chickens
1 cup chopped celery
1 onion, chopped
2 tablespoons butter
2 4-ounce cans
  button mushrooms,
  drained
2 10-ounce cans cream
  of mushroom soup
2 tablespoons soy
  sauce
1/4 cup slivered
  almonds
1 5-ounce can chow
  mein noodles

Rinse chickens inside and out. Cook in water to cover in saucepan until tender. Drain, reserving 3 tablespoons broth. Chop chicken, discarding skin and bones. Sauté celery and onion in butter in skillet. Combine chicken with sautéed vegetables, mushrooms, soup and reserved broth in bowl; mix well. Spoon into baking dish. Top with almonds and noodles. Bake at 350 degrees for 45 minutes. Serve with wild rice and salad of romaine lettuce, eggs, mushrooms and artichoke hearts.

Easy Chicken Kiev

Yield:
4 servings
Utensil:
baking dish

*Approx Per
Serving:*
Cal 420
Prot 32 g
Carbo 12 g
Fiber 1 g
T Fat 27 g
Chol 106 mg
Sod 586 mg

4 chicken breast filets
2 green chili peppers,
  rinsed, seeded
4 1/2-ounce pieces
  Monterey Jack
  cheese
1/2 cup fine dry bread
  crumbs
1/4 cup grated
  Parmesan cheese
1/2 to 1 teaspoon garlic
  powder
1/2 to 1 teaspoon
  parsley flakes
1/2 teaspoon cumin
1/2 teaspoon pepper
3 tablespoons melted
  butter

Rinse chicken and pat dry. Pound 1/4 inch thick with meat mallet. Cut chili peppers into halves. Place 1 piece chili pepper and 1 piece Monterey Jack cheese on each filet. Roll chicken to enclose filling, tucking in sides. Combine bread crumbs, Parmesan cheese, garlic powder, parsley flakes, cumin and pepper in bowl; mix well. Dip chicken rolls into butter; coat with bread crumb mixture. Arrange with sides not touching in 9x13-inch baking dish. Drizzle with remaining butter. Chill in refrigerator for 30 minutes or longer. Bake at 400 degrees for 20 to 25 minutes or until done to taste.

Chicken Fricassee

1½ cups flour
1 teaspoon salt
⅛ teaspoon pepper
3½ pounds cut-up chicken
¼ cup shortening
½ cup chopped celery
¼ cup chopped onion
1 10-ounce can cream of mushroom soup
2 tablespoons chopped pimento
3¼ cups water

Mix flour, salt and pepper together. Rinse chicken and pat dry. Coat with flour mixture. Cook in hot shortening in skillet until tender but not brown. Place chicken in baking dish; drain skillet. Add celery, onion, soup, pimento and water to skillet, stirring to deglaze. Pour over chicken. Bake, covered, at 350 degrees for 1 hour or until tender. Serve with rice.

Honey-Baked Chicken

¼ cup water
1 3-pound chicken
1 12-ounce jar honey

Pour water into baking dish. Rinse chicken and pat dry; place in prepared dish. Drizzle with half the honey. Bake at 375 degrees for 30 minutes. Drizzle remaining honey over chicken. Bake for 1 hour longer, basting with pan drippings every 15 to 30 minutes.

Nutritional information includes entire amount of honey.

Chicken Divan

Yield:
8 servings
Utensil:
baking dish

Approx Per Serving:
Cal 387
Prot 27 g
Carbo 12 g
Fiber 2 g
T Fat 26 g
Chol 85 mg
Sod 628 mg

1 2¹/₂-pound chicken
2 10-ounce packages frozen broccoli spears
1 10-ounce can cream of chicken soup
²/₃ cup mayonnaise
¹/₃ cup milk
1 teaspoon lemon juice
¹/₂ cup finely chopped American cheese
¹/₂ teaspoon curry powder
¹/₂ cup bread crumbs
1 tablespoon melted margarine

Rinse chicken inside and out. Cook in water to cover in saucepan until tender. Remove chicken from bones, discarding skin. Parboil broccoli; drain. Layer broccoli and chicken in 9x13-inch baking dish. Combine soup, mayonnaise, milk, lemon juice, cheese and curry powder in bowl; mix well. Spoon over layers. Top with mixture of bread crumbs and margarine. Bake at 350 degrees for 30 minutes.

Chicken Juliet

Yield:
4 servings
Utensil:
skillet

Approx Per Serving:
Cal 275
Prot 23 g
Carbo 7 g
Fiber 1 g
T Fat 17 g
Chol 92 mg
Sod 788 mg

4 chicken breasts
2 tablespoons butter
1 4-ounce can sliced mushrooms, drained
1 clove of garlic, minced
1 10-ounce can cream of chicken soup
¹/₃ cup light cream

Rinse chicken and pat dry. Brown in butter in large skillet; remove to plate. Stir mushrooms, garlic and soup into skillet. Add chicken. Simmer, covered, for 45 minutes, stirring occasionally. Stir in cream. Heat just to serving temperature.

CHICKEN AND RICE

<table>
<tr><td>

Yield:
4 servings
Utensil:
baking dish

*Approx Per
Serving:*
Cal 325
Prot 26 g
Carbo 32 g
Fiber 4 g
T Fat 10 g
Chol 58 mg
Sod 1753 mg

</td><td>

4 chicken breast
  quarters
1 cup uncooked long
  grain rice
1 4-ounce can
  mushrooms, drained
1 8-ounce can green
  peas, drained

</td><td>

1 10-ounce can cream
  of mushroom soup
1 10-ounce can cream
  of celery soup
2 soup cans water
1/2 envelope onion
  soup mix

</td></tr>
</table>

Rinse chicken and pat dry. Sprinkle rice into 9x13-inch baking dish sprayed with nonstick cooking spray. Layer mushrooms, peas and chicken over rice. Spread soups over chicken. Pour water over layers; sprinkle with soup mix. Bake, covered, at 375 degrees for 45 minutes or until done to taste. May use cut-up chicken or leg quarters if preferred.

CRESCENT CHICKEN SQUARES

<table>
<tr><td>

Yield:
4 servings
Utensil:
baking sheet

*Approx Per
Serving:*
Cal 557
Prot 27 g
Carbo 36 g
Fiber 1 g
T Fat 33 g
Chol 87 mg
Sod 954 mg

</td><td>

3 ounces cream cheese,
  softened
2 tablespoons melted
  margarine
2 cups chopped
  cooked chicken
1 tablespoon chopped
  chives

</td><td>

1/4 teaspoon salt
1/8 teaspoon pepper
1 8-count can
  crescent rolls
1 tablespoon melted
  margarine
3/4 cup seasoned bread
  crumbs

</td></tr>
</table>

Blend cream cheese and 2 tablespoons margarine in medium bowl. Add chicken, chives, salt and pepper; mix well. Separate roll dough into 4 rectangles, pressing diagonal perforations to seal. Spoon chicken mixture into center of each rectangle. Pull up corners of dough to enclose filling, twisting slightly to seal well. Place on baking sheet. Brush tops with 1 tablespoon margarine; sprinkle with bread crumbs. Bake at 350 degrees for 20 to 25 minutes or until golden brown.

CURRIED CHICKEN

Yield:
6 servings
Utensil:
baking dish

**Approx Per
Serving:**
Cal 286
Prot 28 g
Carbo 7 g
Fiber <1 g
T Fat 16 g
Chol 108 mg
Sod 621 mg

²/₃ cup cracker crumbs
2 teaspoons curry
  powder
1 teaspoon onion salt
¹/₈ teaspoon ginger
1 2¹/₂-pound chicken,
  cut up
¹/₄ cup melted butter

Mix cracker crumbs, curry powder, onion salt and ginger on waxed paper. Rinse chicken and pat dry. Brush with butter; coat with crumb mixture. Place skin side up with sides not touching in shallow baking dish. Pierce skin with fork in several places. Bake at 375 degrees for 50 minutes or until juices run clear when chicken is pierced with fork.

LEMON CHICKEN SURPRISE

Yield:
6 servings
Utensil:
baking dish

**Approx Per
Serving:**
Cal 286
Prot 36 g
Carbo 16 g
Fiber 6 g
T Fat 9 g
Chol 101 mg
Sod 323 mg

2 stalks celery,
  chopped
1 small green bell
  pepper, chopped
2 medium onions,
  chopped
2 large carrots,
  chopped
4 ounces mushrooms,
  sliced
1 small eggplant,
  chopped
Salt to taste
1 3-pound chicken,
  skinned
1 lemon
1 chicken bouillon
  cube
Flowerets of 1 head
  cauliflower

Combine celery, green pepper, onions, carrots, mushrooms, eggplant, salt and water to cover in saucepan. Simmer just until vegetables are tender. Drain, reserving cooking liquid. Rinse chicken inside and out and pat dry. Sear on all sides in heavy skillet. Spoon vegetables into chicken cavity. Place in 10-inch baking dish. Squeeze juice from lemon over chicken; place lemon rind in cavity. Dissolve bouillon cube in reserved cooking liquid. Pour into baking dish. Bake at 350 degrees for 1¹/₂ hours or until tender. Cook cauliflower in a small amount of water in saucepan until tender; drain. Place chicken in center of platter; arrange cauliflower around chicken. Spoon some of the pan juices over chicken. Serve with remaining pan juices. Garnish with orange slices and parsley.

Lemon Yogurt Chicken

Yield:
4 servings
Utensil:
baking dish

Approx Per
Serving:
Cal 141
Prot 22 g
Carbo 8 g
Fiber 0 g
T Fat 2 g
Chol 52 mg
Sod 92 mg

8 ounces lemon yogurt
1 teaspoon ginger
1/2 teaspoon garlic
  powder
1/2 teaspoon paprika
1/2 teaspoon coriander
4 chicken breasts,
  skinned

Combine yogurt, ginger, garlic power, paprika and coriander in rectangular 2-quart baking dish. Rinse chicken and pat dry. Add to yogurt mixture, coating well. Marinate in refrigerator for 8 hours to overnight, spooning marinade over chicken occasionally. Bake at 375 degrees for 40 to 50 minutes or until done to taste, basting frequently.

Mexican Chicken Pizza

Yield:
4 servings
Utensil:
pizza pan

Approx Per
Serving:
Cal 323
Prot 15 g
Carbo 33 g
Fiber 1 g
T Fat 14 g
Chol 46 mg
Sod 493 mg

8 ounces chicken
  breast filets
Juice of 1 lime
1 tablespoon chopped
  fresh cilantro
1 can refrigerator
  pizza dough
2/3 cup tomato sauce
2 tablespoons salsa
1/2 cup shredded
  Cheddar cheese
1/2 cup shredded
  mozzarella cheese

Rinse chicken and pat dry. Cut into bite-sized pieces. Combine with lime juice and cilantro in bowl. Marinate, covered, for 15 minutes. Sauté in skillet sprayed with nonstick cooking spray. Place pizza dough in pizza pan, using package directions. Top with tomato sauce, salsa, cheeses and chicken. Bake at 400 degrees for 12 to 15 minutes or until crust is brown.

ORIENTAL CHICKEN

Yield:
6 servings
Utensil:
skillet

Approx Per
Serving:
Cal 266
Prot 18 g
Carbo 45 g
Fiber 6 g
T Fat 1 g
Chol 16 mg
Sod 1086 mg

1/2 cup orange juice
1/2 cup dry red wine
1/2 cup reduced-
    sodium soy sauce
1 large whole chicken
    breast, skinned
1 16-ounce package
    mixed Italian-style
    vegetables
1 10-ounce package
    frozen chopped
    broccoli
8 ounces no-yolk egg
    noodles, cooked

Combine orange juice, wine and soy sauce in bowl. Rinse chicken and pat dry. Cut into bite-sized pieces. Add to marinade; mix well. Marinate in refrigerator for 1 hour. Drain, reserving marinade. Stir-fry chicken in large skillet sprayed with non-stick cooking spray until brown. Add reserved marinade. Simmer for 45 minutes or until tender, adding water as needed for desired consistency. Add mixed vegetables and broccoli. Cook until vegetables are tender. Serve over noodles.

TURKEY CASSEROLE

Yield:
8 servings
Utensil:
baking dish

Approx Per
Serving:
Cal 382
Prot 30 g
Carbo 43 g
Fiber 4 g
T Fat 11 g
Chol 78 mg
Sod 702 mg

2 cups leftover stuffing
8 slices cooked turkey
2 cups turkey gravy
1/2 16-ounce can
    cranberry sauce,
    sliced
Salt and pepper to
    taste
4 cups mashed
    potatoes

Spread stuffing in baking dish. Layer turkey and gravy over stuffing. Arrange cranberry sauce over gravy; sprinkle with salt and pepper. Top with mashed potatoes. Bake at 350 degrees for 30 to 40 minutes or until potatoes are golden brown and casserole is heated through.

GROUND TURKEY GOULASH

Yield:
4 servings
Utensil:
skillet

Approx Per Serving:
Cal 335
Prot 28 g
Carbo 29 g
Fiber 4 g
T Fat 12 g
Chol 72 mg
Sod 1146 mg

1 pound ground turkey
1 32-ounce can tomatoes
1/2 cup chopped green bell pepper
1 4-ounce can mushroom pieces
1 tablespoon onion flakes
2 packets beef or chicken bouillon mix
Onion powder, garlic powder, salt and pepper to taste
3 ounces uncooked elbow macaroni

Brown turkey in nonstick skillet sprayed with non-stick cooking spray, stirring until crumbly. Add tomatoes, green pepper, undrained mushrooms, onion flakes, bouillon, onion powder, garlic powder, salt and pepper; mix well. Bring to a boil. Add pasta. Cook for 20 minutes or until pasta is tender and liquid is absorbed.

GROUND TURKEY SAUSAGE

Yield:
4 servings
Utensil:
skillet

Approx Per Serving:
Cal 191
Prot 22 g
Carbo 0 g
Fiber 0 g
T Fat 11 g
Chol 71 mg
Sod 231 mg

1 pound ground turkey
1/8 teaspoon savory
1/2 teaspoon crushed fennel seed
1/4 teaspoon sage
1/4 teaspoon thyme
1/4 teaspoon marjoram
1/4 teaspoon salt
1/4 teaspoon pepper

Combine ground turkey, savory, fennel seed, sage, thyme, marjoram, salt and pepper in bowl; mix well. Shape into 4 patties. Cook until brown on both sides in skillet.

SEAFOOD

Sailbouts in the Harbor

CREOLE FLOUNDER

Yield:
4 servings
Utensil:
baking dish

Approx Per
Serving:
Cal 113
Prot 18 g
Carbo 4 g
Fiber 1 g
T Fat 3 g
Chol 44 mg
Sod 77 mg

1 pound flounder filets
1 tomato, chopped
1/2 green bell pepper, chopped
3 tablespoons lemon juice
1 1/2 teaspoons oil
1/4 onion, finely chopped
Pepper sauce to taste
1/2 teaspoon basil
1/8 teaspoon pepper

Arrange fish in 9x13-inch baking dish sprayed with nonstick cooking spray. Combine tomato, green pepper, lemon juice, oil, onion, pepper sauce, basil and pepper in bowl; mix well. Spoon over fish. Bake at 400 degrees for 10 minutes or until fish flakes easily.

BAKED HADDOCK

Yield:
4 servings
Utensil:
baking dish

Approx Per
Serving:
Cal 468
Prot 38 g
Carbo 16 g
Fiber <1 g
T Fat 31 g
Chol 101 mg
Sod 596 mg

1 1/2 pounds fresh haddock, skinned
Pepper to taste
Juice of 1 lemon
1/2 cup melted margarine
1 stack butter crackers, finely crushed
Garlic powder, paprika and dillweed to taste

Rinse fish and pat dry; cut into 4 portions. Arrange skinned side down in foil-lined 9x13-inch baking dish, tucking thin ends under. Sprinkle with pepper; drizzle with lemon juice. Spread each filet with 1 teaspoon melted margarine. Combine remaining margarine with cracker crumbs in bowl; mix well. Spoon over fish. Sprinkle with garlic powder, paprika and dillweed. Bake at 350 degrees for 30 minutes or until fish flakes easily. Serve with lemon wedges.

Mom's Salmon Cakes

Yield:
4 servings
Utensil:
skillet

Approx Per
Serving:
Cal 233
Prot 15 g
Carbo 31 g
Fiber 2 g
T Fat 5 g
Chol 75 mg
Sod 291 mg

3 potatoes, peeled
1 7-ounce can red
　　sockeye salmon

1 egg
1/4 cup flour
Oil for frying

Cook potatoes in water to cover in saucepan until tender. Drain and mash potatoes. Flake salmon, discarding skin and bones. Add egg and salmon to potatoes; mix well. Coat with flour. Fry on both sides in oil in skillet until crisp and brown. Serve with beans or rice.

Nutritional information does not include oil for frying.

Stuffed Sole

Yield:
4 servings
Utensil:
baking dish

Approx Per
Serving:
Cal 441
Prot 33 g
Carbo 42 g
Fiber <1 g
T Fat 15 g
Chol 65 mg
Sod 1218 mg

1 8-ounce package
　　stove-top stuffing
　　mix
1 1/2 pounds sole filets
2 tablespoons lemon
　　juice

1/4 cup melted
　　margarine
Pepper to taste

Prepare stuffing mix using package directions. Spoon onto centers of filets; roll to enclose stuffing. Place in greased 8x12-inch baking dish. Drizzle with lemon juice and margarine; sprinkle with pepper. Bake at 400 degrees for 15 minutes or until fish flakes easily. Serve with Hollandaise sauce. May substitute flounder for sole if preferred.

Barbecued Swordfish

Yield:
1 serving
Utensil:
grill

Approx Per Serving:
Cal 556
Prot 47 g
Carbo 6 g
Fiber <1 g
T Fat 45 g
Chol 91 mg
Sod 496 mg

¼ cup Italian salad dressing
1 8-ounce swordfish steak

1 to 2 tablespoons blackened seasoning

Pour salad dressing over steak in bowl. Marinate for 5 minutes; drain. Sprinkle with seasoning. Grill on grill brushed with olive oil for 5 minutes on each side or until done to taste; do not overcook.

Nutritional information does not include blackened seasoning.

Summer Tuna Cakes

Yield:
2 servings
Utensil:
sauté pan

Approx Per Serving:
Cal 593
Prot 43 g
Carbo 57 g
Fiber 4 g
T Fat 21 g
Chol 166 mg
Sod 1208 mg

1 zucchini
1 7-ounce can tuna
1½ cups bread cubes
1 egg
2 teaspoons grated onion

¼ teaspoon lemon juice
¼ teaspoon salt
¼ teaspoon pepper
2 tablespoons oil

Shred zucchini; pat dry with paper towels. Combine with tuna, bread cubes, egg, onion, lemon juice, salt and pepper in bowl; mix well. Shape into 2 patties. Cook in oil in sauté pan over medium heat for 8 to 10 minutes or until brown on both sides.

Quick Clam Linguine

Yield:
2 servings
Utensil:
sauté pan

Approx Per Serving:
Cal 720
Prot 23 g
Carbo 91 g
Fiber 5 g
T Fat 35 g
Chol 63 mg
Sod 46 mg

4 or 5 cloves of garlic, minced
1/4 cup olive oil
1 7-ounce can minced clams
1 teaspoon chopped parsley
8 ounces linguine, cooked

Sauté garlic in olive oil in sauté pan until tender but not brown. Drain clams, reserving liquid. Add reserved clam liquid and parsley to sauté pan. Simmer for 10 minutes; remove from heat. Stir in clams. Heat just until heated through. Serve over linguine.

White Clam Sauce with Pasta

Yield:
4 servings
Utensil:
saucepan

Approx Per Serving:
Cal 636
Prot 25 g
Carbo 95 g
Fiber 5 g
T Fat 22 g
Chol 71 mg
Sod 206 mg

1 large clove of garlic, minced
1/4 cup margarine
2 tablespoons flour
2 7-ounce cans minced clams
1/4 cup dry white wine
1 cup (about) milk
1/4 cup finely chopped parsley
1/2 teaspoon thyme
Salt and pepper to taste
1 16-ounce package linguine, cooked

Sauté garlic in margarine in small saucepan. Stir in flour. Cook for 2 minutes. Drain clams, reserving liquid. Combine reserved clam liquid with wine and enough milk to measure 2 cups. Add to saucepan gradually. Cook until thickened, stirring constantly. Add parsley, thyme, salt and pepper. Simmer for 10 minutes. Add clams. Cook until heated through. Serve over linguine.

SCALLOPED CLAMS

Yield:
4 servings
Utensil:
baking dish

Approx Per Serving:
Cal 318
Prot 8 g
Carbo 10 g
Fiber <1 g
T Fat 31 g
Chol 158 mg
Sod 354 mg

1 cup milk
1/2 cup butter
10 crackers, crumbled
1 pint minced clams
1 egg
Salt and pepper to
  taste

Scald milk in saucepan. Add butter, cracker crumbs, clams, egg, salt and pepper; mix well. Spoon into 8x8-inch baking dish. Bake at 375 degrees for 40 minutes.

BAKED LOBSTER

Yield:
4 servings
Utensil:
baking sheet

Approx Per Serving:
Cal 1039
Prot 75 g
Carbo 48 g
Fiber 1 g
T Fat 67 g
Chol 244 mg
Sod 2539 mg

4 1½-pound lobsters
2 tablespoons chopped
  parsley
2 cloves of garlic,
  minced
1 small onion, chopped
1 cup margarine
3 stacks butter
  crackers, crushed
Pepper to taste

Split lobsters from head to tip of tail with sharp knife. Discard intestinal vein and stomach; leave tomalleys in place. Place on baking sheet. Sauté parsley, garlic and onion in margarine in skillet. Add cracker crumbs and pepper. Spoon into cavities in lobsters. Cover claws with foil. Bake at 450 degrees for 15 to 20 minutes or until done to taste.

LOBSTER NEWBURG

Yield:
6 servings
Utensil:
saucepan

Approx Per
Serving:
Cal 366
Prot 14 g
Carbo 10 g
Fiber 1 g
T Fat 30 g
Chol 263 mg
Sod 1068 mg

2 10-ounce cans cream of shrimp soup
1¹/₂ cups heavy cream
4 egg yolks, beaten
10 ounces lobster meat
2 4-ounce cans sliced mushrooms, drained
3 tablespoons Marsala

Combine soup, cream, egg yolks, lobster, mushrooms and wine in saucepan. Bring to a boil; reduce heat. Simmer, covered, for 1¹/₂ hours, stirring occasionally. Serve over rice, egg noodles, chow mein noodles or in puff pastry shells. May add peas if desired.

LOBSTER THERMIDOR

Yield:
2 servings
Utensil:
baking sheet

Approx Per
Serving:
Cal 586
Prot 41 g
Carbo 16 g
Fiber 1 g
T Fat 39 g
Chol 230 mg
Sod 3603 mg

2 teaspoons lemon juice
2 teaspoons salt
4 lobster tails
¹/₄ cup chopped green onions
1 to 2 tablespoons parsley flakes
¹/₄ cup butter
2 tablespoons flour
2 tablespoons dry mustard
¹/₂ teaspoon salt
¹/₄ teaspoon pepper
1 cup half and half
1 tablespoon dry sherry
2 teaspoons grated Parmesan cheese
2 teaspoons fine dry bread crumbs

Fill large heavy saucepan half full with water. Add lemon juice and 2 teaspoons salt. Bring to a boil. Add lobster tails. Return to a boil. Cook for 3 to 6 minutes or until lobster is firm and opaque. Drain and cool. Remove meat with sharp knife or scissors; reserve shells. Chop meat, discarding membrane. Sauté green onions and parsley flakes in butter in medium saucepan over medium-high heat. Stir in flour, dry mustard, ¹/₂ teaspoon salt and pepper. Add half and half. Cook just until thickened, stirring constantly. Stir in wine and lobster meat. Spoon into reserved shells; place on baking sheet. Top with mixture of Parmesan cheese and bread crumbs. Bake at 375 degrees for 15 to 20 minutes or until heated through.

BAKED STUFFED SCALLOPS

Yield:
4 servings
Utensil:
baking dish

Approx Per
Serving:
Cal 459
Prot 44 g
Carbo 22 g
Fiber 1 g
T Fat 23 g
Chol 127 mg
Sod 700 mg

2 pounds bay or sea
  scallops
2 tablespoons butter
1/2 cup seasoned bread
  crumbs

1/2 cup finely crushed
  butter crackers
1/4 cup melted butter

Place scallops in baking dish; dot with 2 tablespoons butter. Bake at 325 degrees for 10 minutes. Combine bread crumbs, cracker crumbs and 1/4 cup melted butter in bowl; mix well. Stir scallops. Add crumb mixture. Bake for 15 minutes longer. Broil for 1 minute.

SCALLOPED SCALLOPS

Yield:
4 servings
Utensil:
baking dish

Approx Per
Serving:
Cal 485
Prot 13 g
Carbo 19 g
Fiber <1 g
T Fat 43 g
Chol 126 mg
Sod 526 mg

1 pint bay or sea
  scallops
1 cup cracker crumbs
1/2 cup soft bread
  crumbs

1/2 cup melted butter
Salt and pepper to
  taste
2/3 cup light cream

Cut large scallops into smaller pieces. Combine cracker crumbs, bread crumbs and melted butter in bowl; mix well. Alternate layers of scallops and crumb mixture in shallow baking dish until all ingredients are used, ending with crumbs. Sprinkle with salt and pepper. Pour cream over layers. Bake at 350 degrees for 30 minutes. Serve immediately.

Scallops in Honey and Butter

Yield:
2 servings
Utensil:
baking dish

Approx Per
Serving:
Cal 548
Prot 43 g
Carbo 25 g
Fiber <1 g
T Fat 34 g
Chol 111 mg
Sod 664 mg

1 pound scallops
1/2 cup butter cracker
  crumbs
1 1/2 teaspoons honey

2 tablespoons melted
  butter
2 tablespoons oil

Cut scallops into halves. Coat with cracker crumbs; place in greased baking dish. Combine honey, butter and oil in bowl; mix well. Drizzle evenly over scallops. Bake at 475 degrees for 10 to 15 minutes or until done to taste. May use bread crumbs or sprinkle additional crumbs over top of casserole.

Garlic Lovers Scampi

Yield:
2 servings
Utensil:
skillet

Approx Per
Serving:
Cal 840
Prot 59 g
Carbo 7 g
Fiber 1 g
T Fat 59 g
Chol 655 mg
Sod 1005 mg

1/3 cup chopped onion
1/4 cup chopped fresh
  parsley
4 to 6 cloves of garlic,
  crushed
1/8 teaspoon white
  pepper

1/2 cup butter
4 1/2 teaspoons olive oil
1 1/4 to 1 1/2 pounds
  large shrimp,
  peeled, deveined
1/3 cup cooking sherry
Juice of 1/2 lemon

Sauté onion, parsley, garlic and pepper in butter and olive oil in large skillet over medium heat for 5 to 6 minutes. Add shrimp. Cook until bubbly. Add wine and lemon juice. Cook over medium heat for 20 to 25 minutes or until sauce thickens, stirring frequently. Serve immediately over rice. Garnish with finely chopped scallions.

Fettucini Galilee

2 ounces scallops
3 jumbo shrimp,
    peeled, chopped
1 tablespoon oil
1 ounce brandy
Chopped shallots and
    garlic to taste
1/2 tomato, chopped
2 scallions, chopped
1 cup heavy cream
1/2 cup grated Romano
    cheese
4 littleneck clams
4 ounces spinach
    fettucini, cooked
4 ounces plain
    fettucini, cooked

Sauté scallops and shrimp in oil in sauté pan. Add brandy. Ignite with match; allow flames to die down. Add shallots, garlic, tomato and scallions. Stir in cream. Bring to a boil; remove from heat. Stir in cheese. Steam clams in saucepan until shells open. Place pasta on serving platter. Pour warm seafood sauce over top; arrange clams around edge. Garnish with parsley and additional Romano cheese.

Bob Goulet's Special Seafood Casserole

8 ounces crab meat
1 pound fresh scallops
1 pound frozen peeled
    shrimp
1/2 cup melted butter
1/2 cup baking mix
1 1/2 cups light cream
Minced onion to taste
3 eggs
Garlic powder, salt
    and pepper to taste
1 cup shredded
    Cheddar cheese

Combine crab meat, scallops and shrimp in 9x13-inch baking dish. Combine butter, baking mix, cream, onion, eggs, garlic powder, salt and pepper in blender container; process until smooth. Pour over seafood. Sprinkle with cheese; press into batter. Bake at 350 degrees for 45 minutes. May substitute lobster for shrimp if preferred.

VEGETABLES
AND SIDE DISHES

The Beach
Nantucket, Massachusetts

BOSTON BAKED BEANS

<table>
<tr><td>

Yield:
8 servings
Utensil:
slow cooker

</td><td>

1 pound dried kidney
  beans
6 cups water
1/2 cup maple syrup
2 teaspoons dry
  mustard

</td><td>

1 medium onion,
  chopped
1 pound bacon,
  chopped
1 teaspoon salt

</td></tr>
</table>

Approx Per Serving:
Cal 369
Prot 19 g
Carbo 55 g
Fiber 13 g
T Fat 9 g
Chol 14 mg
Sod 558 mg

1/4 cup packed brown
  sugar

Combine beans with water in slow cooker. Let stand for 6 hours to overnight. Cook on High for 2 to 3 hours or until beans are tender. Drain, reserving cooking liquid. Combine reserved liquid with syrup, dry mustard, brown sugar, onion, bacon and salt in bowl. Combine with beans in slow cooker. Cook on Low for 10 to 12 hours or until done to taste.

MAUDE DUSTON'S SAWMILL CAMP BAKED BEANS

<table>
<tr><td>

Yield:
10 servings
Utensil:
beanpot

</td><td>

1 pound dried navy
  pea beans
1/2 cup packed brown
  sugar

</td><td>

1/4 cup dark molasses
1/2 teaspoon soda
Dry mustard to taste
4 ounces lean salt pork

</td></tr>
</table>

Approx Per Serving:
Cal 230
Prot 11 g
Carbo 43 g
Fiber 1 g
T Fat 2 g
Chol 3 mg
Sod 113 mg

Soak beans in cold water to cover in saucepan overnight. Bring to a boil in same water. Cook until skins of beans begin to split. Combine undrained beans, brown sugar, molasses, soda and dry mustard in 2-quart beanpot. Slice salt pork into thick strips. Add to beanpot; mix well. Bake, covered, at 275 to 300 degrees for 6 to 8 hours or until beans are tender. Add water as needed to prevent beans drying out. May substitute kidney beans for navy beans, increase brown sugar to 3/4 cup and omit molasses. This recipe has been handed down through 6 generations of native Yankees and was used to feed hungry sawyers in busy sawmill camps in New England in the early 1900s.

GREEN BEAN CASSEROLE

Yield:
4 servings
Utensil:
glass dish

Approx Per Serving:
Cal 103
Prot 5 g
Carbo 11 g
Fiber 3 g
T Fat 5 g
Chol 8 mg
Sod 158 mg

1 pound fresh green beans
1 medium onion, sliced
6 slices bacon, chopped
Pepper to taste

Combine green beans with onion, bacon and pepper in glass dish. Microwave, covered, on High for 13 minutes, stirring after 5 minutes.

BOURADSKI (Creamed Beets)

Yield:
6 servings
Utensil:
saucepan

Approx Per Serving:
Cal 137
Prot 2 g
Carbo 16 g
Fiber 1 g
T Fat 8 g
Chol 17 mg
Sod 231

8 medium fresh beets
1/2 cup water
1/2 cup white vinegar
1/4 cup sugar
1/2 teaspoon salt
1 cup sour cream

Cook beets in water in saucepan for 25 minutes; drain. Cool, peel and grate beets. Blend 1/4 cup water, vinegar, sugar and salt in saucepan. Bring to a boil. Let cool slightly. Add beets. Add sour cream gradually, mixing to desired consistency. Serve warm or cool. May drain part of the vinegar mixture prior to adding sour cream if mixture appears thinner than desired.

CHEESY BROCCOLI AND CAULIFLOWER BAKE

Yield:
10 servings
Utensil:
baking dish

Approx Per Serving:
Cal 177
Prot 6 g
Carbo 17 g
Fiber 4 g
T Fat 10 g
Chol 19 mg
Sod 271 mg

1½ pounds broccoli, chopped
1½ pounds cauliflower, chopped
Salt to taste
½ cup low-fat milk
1 10-ounce can reduced-sodium cream of mushroom soup
½ cup shredded Cheddar cheese
1 cup baking mix
¼ cup butter

Add broccoli and cauliflower to salted boiling water in saucepan. Cook until tender-crisp; drain. Place in 9x13-inch baking dish. Combine milk and soup in small bowl; mix well. Pour over vegetables; sprinkle with cheese. Combine baking mix and butter in bowl; mix until crumbly. Sprinkle over cheese. Bake at 400 degrees for 25 minutes. May omit broccoli or cauliflower and bake in 8x8-inch baking dish if preferred.

BROCCOLI TIMBALE

Yield:
6 servings
Utensil:
ring mold

Approx Per Serving:
Cal 155
Prot 9 g
Carbo 5 g
Fiber 1 g
T Fat 12 g
Chol 167 mg
Sod 310 mg

Paprika to taste
3 cups chopped fresh broccoli
½ cup shredded Cheddar cheese
4 eggs, beaten
1 cup half and half
¼ teaspoon dry mustard
¼ teaspoon lemon pepper
¼ teaspoon onion powder
Cayenne pepper to taste
½ teaspoon salt

Grease 4-cup ring mold. Sprinkle with paprika, coating well. Bring broccoli and water to cover to a boil in medium saucepan; reduce heat. Cook, covered, for 3 minutes; drain. Place in prepared mold; sprinkle with cheese. Beat eggs with half and half, dry mustard, lemon pepper, onion powder, cayenne pepper and salt in bowl. Pour over broccoli. Place ring mold in 10x10-inch baking dish. Add hot water to depth of 1 inch. Bake at 325 degrees for 35 to 40 minutes or until knife inserted in center comes out clean. Invert onto serving plate.

CREAMY CAULIFLOWER BAKE

Yield:
6 servings
Utensil:
baking dish

Approx Per
Serving:
Cal 263
Prot 6 g
Carbo 21 g
Fiber 1 g
T Fat 18 g
Chol 12 mg
Sod 806 mg

Flowerets of 1 medium head cauliflower
1 10-ounce can cream of mushroom soup
1/4 cup milk
1/2 cup shredded Cheddar cheese
1/4 cup margarine
1 cup baking mix

Cook cauliflower in water to cover in saucepan for 10 to 12 minutes or until tender-crisp; drain. Place in ungreased round 1½-quart baking dish. Combine soup and milk in bowl; beat with rotary beater until smooth. Spread over cauliflower. Sprinkle with cheese. Mix margarine and baking mix in bowl until crumbly. Sprinkle over casserole. Bake at 400 degrees for 20 minutes or until topping is light brown. May substitute broccoli for cauliflower.

LAZY PIEROGI

Yield:
10 servings
Utensil:
baking dish

Approx Per
Serving:
Cal 375
Prot 8 g
Carbo 41 g
Fiber 2 g
T Fat 21 g
Chol 50 mg
Sod 764 mg

1 large onion, chopped
1 cup butter
2 pounds sauerkraut
1/2 teaspoon caraway seed
1/2 teaspoon parsley flakes
3 tablespoons brown sugar
Pepper to taste
1 pound uncooked kluski noodles

Sauté onion lightly in butter in saucepan. Rinse sauerkraut under cold water; drain well. Add to onion with caraway seed, parsley flakes, brown sugar and pepper; mix well. Simmer for 10 to 15 minutes. Cook noodles using package directions; drain. Add to sauerkraut; mix well. Spoon into baking dish. Bake, covered, at 350 degrees for 30 minutes. May add 1 pound cooked kielbasa for one-dish meal.

DELICIOUS MASHED POTATOES

<table>
<tr><td>

Yield:
10 servings
Utensil:
baking dish

Approx Per Serving:
Cal 283
Prot 6 g
Carbo 35 g
Fiber 2 g
T Fat 14 g
Chol 37 mg
Sod 1407 mg

</td><td>

10 large potatoes, peeled, chopped
6 ounces cream cheese, softened
1 cup sour cream
2 tablespoons salt
1/4 teaspoon pepper
1/4 cup grated Parmesan cheese
2 tablespoons butter

</td></tr>
</table>

Cook potatoes in water to cover in saucepan until tender; drain and mash. Combine with cream cheese, sour cream, salt and pepper in bowl; mix well. Spoon into buttered 2-quart baking dish. Chill, covered, for 3 days or longer. Sprinkle with Parmesan cheese; dot with butter. Bake at 350 degrees for 45 minutes.

FRENCH-STYLE POTATOES

<table>
<tr><td>

Yield:
6 servings
Utensil:
baking dish

Approx Per Serving:
Cal 261
Prot 4 g
Carbo 37 g
Fiber 3 g
T Fat 12 g
Chol 0 mg
Sod 9 mg

</td><td>

2 pounds potatoes, peeled, sliced
Salt to taste
1 medium onion, chopped
2 tablespoons flour
1/4 cup olive oil
2 tablespoons chopped parsley
Grated rind of 1 lemon
1/4 teaspoon nutmeg
Salt and pepper to taste
1 tablespoon olive oil
Juice of 1 lemon

</td></tr>
</table>

Parboil potatoes in salted water in saucepan for 3 minutes; drain. Combine onion, flour, 1/4 cup olive oil, parsley, lemon rind, nutmeg, salt and pepper in bowl; mix well. Add potatoes; mix gently. Spoon into buttered baking dish. Drizzle with 1 tablespoon olive oil. Bake at 450 degrees for 20 to 25 minutes or until brown. Drizzle with lemon juice. Serve immediately.

Garlic Potatoes

Yield:
6 servings
Utensil:
baking sheet

Approx Per
Serving:
Cal 297
Prot 5 g
Carbo 53 g
Fiber 5 g
T Fat 8 g
Chol 0 mg
Sod 106 mg

6 potatoes
1 onion, sliced
Garlic salt to taste

¹/₄ cup margarine,
    softened

Place potatoes on foil-lined baking sheet; cut each potato into 4 quarters. Top with onion; sprinkle with garlic salt. Spread with margarine. Bake at 350 degrees for 20 to 30 minutes or until tender.

Twice-Baked Potatoes

Yield:
4 servings
Utensil:
baking sheet

Approx Per
Serving:
Cal 404
Prot 7 g
Carbo 52 g
Fiber 5 g
T Fat 19 g
Chol 49 mg
Sod 530 mg

4 potatoes
¹/₃ cup butter
¹/₄ cup milk
1 teaspoon
    freeze-dried chives
1 teaspoon parlsey
    flakes

2 tablespoons
    crumbled crisp-
    fried bacon
¹/₂ teaspoon salt
¹/₄ teaspoon pepper
Paprika to taste

Bake potatoes at 375 degrees until tender. Cut narrow lengthwise slice from each potato. Scoop out potato pulp, reserving ¹/₄-inch shells. Combine potato pulp with butter in mixer bowl. Beat at low speed until butter melts. Add milk, chives, parsley flakes, bacon, salt and pepper. Beat at high speed until smooth. Spoon into reserved shells. Place on baking sheet; sprinkle with paprika. Bake at 375 degrees for 30 minutes.

TWICE-BAKED SOUR CREAM POTATOES

Yield:
12 servings
Utensil:
baking sheet

Approx Per
Serving:
Cal 290
Prot 7 g
Carbo 28 g
Fiber 4 g
T Fat 17 g
Chol 41 mg
Sod 359 mg

6 medium potatoes
1 cup sour cream
1/2 cup butter
1/2 cup grated
   Parmesan cheese
1 envelope onion soup
   mix

1/2 cup bacon bits
1 cup shredded
   Monterey Jack
   cheese
3 green onions,
   chopped

Bake potatoes at 400 degrees until tender. Slice potatoes into halves lengthwise. Scoop potato pulp into large bowl, reserving shells. Add sour cream, butter, Parmesan cheese, soup mix and bacon bits to potato pulp; mix well. Spoon into reserved shells. Place on baking sheet; top with Monterey Jack cheese and green onions. Bake at 400 degrees for 15 minutes or until cheese melts.

SPINACH NEAPOLITAN

Yield:
4 servings
Utensil:
baking dish

Approx Per
Serving:
Cal 377
Prot 25 g
Carbo 28 g
Fiber 4 g
T Fat 19 g
Chol 154 mg
Sod 1249 mg

2 eggs
2 cups milk
1 teaspoon salt
2 10-ounce packages
   frozen chopped
   spinach, thawed

1/2 to 3/4 cup bread
   crumbs
1 1/2 cups shredded
   provolone cheese
Paprika to taste

Beat eggs with milk and salt in bowl. Press spinach to remove moisture. Add spinach, bread crumbs and half the cheese to egg mixture; mix well. Spoon into buttered 1 1/2-quart baking dish. Sprinkle remaining cheese around edge of dish. Sprinkle with paprika. Bake at 375 degrees for 30 to 35 minutes or until bubbly.

SPICED SWEET POTATO BALLS

Yield:
6 servings
Utensil:
deep-fryer

**Approx Per
Serving:**
*Cal 244
Prot 3 g
Carbo 21 g
Fiber 3 g
T Fat 17 g
Chol 10 mg
Sod 394 mg*

3 large sweet potatoes
1 cup chopped pecans
1/8 teaspoon cinnamon
1/8 teaspoon nutmeg
1/8 teaspoon allspice

2 tablespoons butter
1 teaspoon salt
1/4 cup flour
Oil for deep frying

Cook sweet potatoes in water to cover in saucepan until tender; drain and peel. Mash in bowl while hot. Add pecans, cinnamon, nutmeg, allspice, butter and salt; mix well. Shape into balls. Coat lightly with flour. Deep-fry in 380-degree oil until golden brown.

Nutritional information does not include oil for deep frying.

ZUCCHINI CASSEROLE

Yield:
8 servings
Utensil:
baking dish

**Approx Per
Serving:**
*Cal 240
Prot 6 g
Carbo 23 g
Fiber 2 g
T Fat 15 g
Chol 9 mg
Sod 655 mg*

4 medium zucchini,
    sliced 1/2 inch thick
Salt to taste
3/4 cup shredded carrot
1/2 cup chopped onion
1/4 cup margarine
1/2 cup sour cream

1   10-ounce can cream
    of chicken soup
2 1/4 cups herb-flavored
    stuffing mix
2 tablespoons melted
    margarine

Cook zucchini in salted water in saucepan for 20 minutes; drain. Sauté carrot and onion in 1/4 cup margarine in saucepan until tender; remove from heat. Stir in sour cream, soup and 1 1/2 cups stuffing mix. Add zucchini; mix gently. Spoon into 1 1/2-quart baking dish. Toss remaining 3/4 cup stuffing mix with 2 tablespoons melted margarine in bowl. Sprinkle over casserole. Bake at 350 degrees for 30 to 40 minutes or until bubbly.

ZUCCHINI PIE

3 cups grated zucchini
4 eggs
1/2 cup oil
1 cup baking mix
1 teaspoon parsley
1/2 teaspoon salt

3 ounces cream cheese, softened
1/4 cup bread crumbs
1/2 cup shredded Cheddar cheese

Combine zucchini, eggs, oil, baking mix, parsley, salt and cream cheese in bowl; mix well. Spoon into greased pie plate. Top with bread crumbs and shredded cheese. Bake at 350 degrees for 30 minutes. Cool slightly to serve.

ZUCCHINI TORTE

3 cups chopped zucchini
1 onion, chopped
1 cup shredded extra-sharp Cheddar cheese

3 eggs, beaten
1 cup baking mix
Salt and pepper to taste

Combine zucchini, onion and cheese in bowl; mix well. Mix in eggs. Add baking mix, salt and pepper; mix well. Spoon into lightly greased 9x9-inch baking dish. Bake at 350 degrees for 45 minutes or until top is brown. Cut into squares. Serve hot or cool.

GOLDEN VEGETABLE BAKE

Yield:
8 servings
Utensil:
baking dish

Approx Per Serving:
Cal 94
Prot 7 g
Carbo 6 g
Fiber 3 g
T Fat 5 g
Chol 64 mg
Sod 248 mg

4 cups chopped cauliflower
1   10-ounce package frozen Brussels sprouts
1/2 teaspoon sugar
1/4 teaspoon rosemary
1/2 teaspoon celery salt
3/4 cup shredded Swiss cheese

2 egg whites
2 egg yolks
2 teaspoons milk
1/8 teaspoon salt
1/8 teaspoon pepper
2 tablespoons grated Parmesan cheese

Bring cauliflower to a boil in water to cover in medium saucepan; reduce heat. Simmer, covered, for 5 to 10 minutes or until tender; drain. Combine with Brussels sprouts, sugar, rosemary and celery salt in bowl; mix well. Spoon into greased 1½-quart baking dish. Sprinkle with Swiss cheese. Beat egg whites in mixer bowl until stiff peaks form. Beat egg yolks with milk, salt and pepper in bowl until thick and lemon-colored. Fold into egg whites with Parmesan cheese. Spread over casserole. Bake at 350 degrees for 15 minutes or until golden brown.

CRANAPPLE CASSEROLE

Yield:
10 servings
Utensil:
baking dish

Approx Per Serving:
Cal 369
Prot 3 g
Carbo 56 g
Fiber 3 g
T Fat 16 g
Chol 25 mg
Sod 161 mg

3 cups chopped peeled apples
2 cups cranberries
2 tablespoons flour
1 cup sugar
3/4 cup chopped pecans
1/2 cup flour

3 envelopes cinnamon-flavored instant oatmeal mix
1/2 cup packed light brown sugar
1/2 cup melted butter

Combine apples, cranberries and 2 tablespoons flour in bowl; toss to coat well. Stir in sugar. Spoon into greased 2-quart baking dish. Mix pecans, 1/2 cup flour, oatmeal mix and brown sugar in bowl. Add margarine; mix until crumbly. Sprinkle over fruit. Bake at 350 degrees for 45 minutes.

FETTUCINI ALFREDO

Yield:
4 servings
Utensil:
saucepan

Approx Per
Serving:
Cal 558
Prot 17 g
Carbo 45 g
Fiber 2 g
T Fat 34 g
Chol 97 mg
Sod 467 mg

8 ounces uncooked
  fettucini
2 tablespoons
  margarine
1 cup whipping cream

1 cup grated Parmesan
  cheese
Salt and pepper to
  taste

Cook pasta using package directions; drain. Combine with margarine in saucepan. Cook over low heat until margarine melts. Add cream gradually, stirring constantly. Add cheese gradually, stirring constantly. Cook over medium heat until thickened. Season with salt and pepper.

FETTUCINI PRIMAVERA

Yield:
4 servings
Utensil:
saucepan

Approx Per
Serving:
Cal 565
Prot 17 g
Carbo 47 g
Fiber 3 g
T Fat 35 g
Chol 97 mg
Sod 472 mg

2 cups mixed chopped
  broccoli, carrots,
  scallions and
  mushrooms
8 ounces uncooked
  fettucini

2 tablespoons
  margarine
1 cup heavy cream
1 cup grated Parmesan
  cheese
Salt and pepper to taste

Combine broccoli, carrots, scallions and mushrooms with a small amount of water in shallow glass dish. Microwave on High for 5 minutes or just until tender; drain. Cook pasta using package directions; drain. Combine with margarine in saucepan. Cook over low heat until margarine melts. Add cream gradually, stirring constantly. Add cheese gradually, stirring constantly. Increase heat to medium. Cook until thickened to desired consistency. Add vegetables, salt and pepper; toss to mix well.

GERMAN NOODLE PUDDING

Yield:
8 servings
Utensil:
baking dish

Approx Per
Serving:
Cal 596
Prot 10 g
Carbo 68 g
Fiber <1 g
T Fat 33 g
Chol 162 mg
Sod 388 mg

8 ounces uncooked
  broad egg noodles
1/2 cup butter
4 ounces cream cheese,
  softened
1 cup milk
1 cup orange juice
3 eggs

3/4 cup sugar
1/2 teaspoon cinnamon
1/2 cup raisins
1/2 cup melted butter
1 cup crushed frosted
  cornflakes
1 1/2 teaspoons
  cinnamon

Cook noodles using package directions; drain. Toss with 1/2 cup butter in bowl. Combine cream cheese, milk, orange juice, eggs, sugar and 1/2 teaspoon cinnamon in small bowl; mix well. Add to noodles. Add raisins; mix well. Spoon into greased 9x13-inch baking dish. Combine 1/2 cup melted butter, cereal and 1 1/2 teaspoons cinnamon in bowl; mix well. Sprinkle over casserole. Bake at 350 degrees for 1 hour. Let stand, covered with foil, for 10 minutes before serving.

ITALIAN GREEN RICE

Yield:
6 servings
Utensil:
saucepan

Approx Per
Serving:
Cal 371
Prot 8 g
Carbo 53 g
Fiber 2 g
T Fat 14 g
Chol 11 mg
Sod 900 mg

1 cup chopped onion
  or scallions
1 cup chopped parsley
1 1/2 cups chopped
  fresh spinach
2 tablespoons olive oil
2 tablespoons butter

2 cups uncooked rice
1 teaspoon salt
Pepper to taste
3 1/2 cups hot chicken
  stock
2 tablespoons butter

Cook onion, parsley and spinach in olive oil and 2 tablespoons butter in tightly covered saucepan over low heat for 5 minutes. Add rice. Cook until rice is translucent, stirring constantly. Add salt, pepper and 2 cups chicken stock. Simmer, covered, for 10 minutes. Add remaining 1 1/2 cups chicken stock. Simmer, covered, for 10 minutes. Add 2 tablespoons butter, mixing lightly with fork. Spoon into serving bowl. Garnish with pepper and Parmesan cheese. Omit salt if using chicken bouillon.

Oven Rice

Yield:
4 servings
Utensil:
baking dish

Approx Per Serving:
Cal 60
Prot 2 g
Carbo 13 g
Fiber <1 g
T Fat 0 g
Chol 0 mg
Sod 798 mg

1 cup long grain rice   **1 teaspoon salt**
2½ cups water

Sprinkle rice into 1-quart baking dish. Add water and salt. Bake, covered, at 350 degrees for 30 minutes. Fluff with fork. Bake, covered, for 20 to 30 minutes longer or until tender.

Rice Pilaf

Yield:
4 servings
Utensil:
saucepan

Approx Per Serving:
Cal 325
Prot 7 g
Carbo 45 g
Fiber 1 g
T Fat 13 g
Chol 32 mg
Sod 1021 mg

1 small onion, chopped   **2 cups chicken broth**
¼ cup uncooked orzo   **1 teaspoon salt**
¼ cup butter   **⅛ teaspoon pepper**
1 cup uncooked rice

Sauté onion and pasta in butter in 2-quart saucepan until pasta is golden brown. Add rice. Sauté for 5 minutes. Add chicken broth, salt and pepper. Bring to a boil. Reduce heat. Simmer, covered, for 20 to 30 minutes or until rice is tender.

BREADS

A New England Shore

COFFEE CAKE

Yield:
15 servings
Utensil:
baking dish

Approx Per
Serving:
Cal 449
Prot 6 g
Carbo 48 g
Fiber 1 g
T Fat 27 g
Chol 83 mg
Sod 383 mg

16 ounces sour cream
2 eggs
8 ounces plain yogurt
1¹/₂ teaspoons vanilla
  extract
¹/₄ cup shredded
  Cheddar cheese
2 tablespoons oil
1 cup melted butter
2¹/₂ cups flour
1¹/₄ cups sugar
2 tablespoons baking
  powder

1¹/₂ teaspoons soda
Salt to taste
¹/₂ cup sugar
¹/₄ cup (heaping) flour
¹/₄ cup packed brown
  sugar
1 teaspoon cinnamon
¹/₂ cup chopped pecans
2¹/₂ tablespoons
  butter, softened

Combine sour cream, eggs and yogurt in bowl; mix well. Add vanilla, cheese, oil and 1 cup butter; mix well. Mix 2¹/₂ cups flour, 1¹/₄ cups sugar, baking powder, soda and salt in bowl. Add to sour cream mixture; mix well. Spoon into greased 9x13-inch baking dish. Combine ¹/₂ cup sugar, ¹/₄ cup flour, brown sugar, cinnamon, pecans and 2¹/₂ tablespoons butter in bowl; mix until crumbly. Sprinkle over batter. Bake at 350 degrees for 40 minutes or until wooden pick inserted in center comes out clean.

SOUR CREAM COFFEE CAKE

Yield:
16 servings
Utensil:
tube pan

Approx Per
Serving:
Cal 249
Prot 3 g
Carbo 27 g
Fiber 1 g
T Fat 15 g
Chol 33 mg
Sod 156 mg

¹/₂ cup margarine,
  softened
1 cup sugar
2 eggs
2 cups flour
1 teaspoon baking
  powder

1 teaspoon soda
1 cup sour cream
2 teaspoons cinnamon
2 teaspoons sugar
1 cup chopped pecans

Cream margarine and 1 cup sugar in mixer bowl until light and fluffy. Beat in eggs. Mix flour, baking powder and soda in bowl. Add to creamed mixture alternately with sour cream, mixing well after each addition. Sprinkle mixture of cinnamon and 2 teaspoons sugar on batter. Swirl lightly into batter. Layer batter and pecans ¹/₂ at a time in greased and floured tube pan. Bake at 350 degrees for 45 minutes. Cool in pan for 10 minutes. Remove to wire rack or serving plate.

SGT. MUNCHING MARGIE'S COFFEE CAKE

Yield:
20 servings
Utensil:
baking pan

Approx Per
Serving:
Cal 288
Prot 4 g
Carbo 42 g
Fiber 2 g
T Fat 13 g
Chol 35 mg
Sod 179 mg

2 eggs
1½ cups sugar
1   16-ounce can fruit
    cocktail
2¼ cups flour
1½ teaspoons soda
½ teaspoon salt
1 teaspoon vanilla
    extract

1¼ cups flaked
    coconut
1 cup chopped walnuts
¾ cup sugar
½ cup butter
¼ cup evaporated milk
½ teaspoon vanilla
    extract
½ cup chopped walnuts

Beat eggs with 1½ cups sugar in mixer bowl until thick and lemon-colored. Add fruit cocktail, flour, soda, salt and 1 teaspoon vanilla; beat at medium speed until smooth. Spoon into greased and floured 10x15-inch baking pan. Sprinkle with coconut and 1 cup walnuts. Bake at 350 degrees for 25 minutes or until coffee cake tests done. Combine ¾ cup sugar, butter, evaporated milk and ½ teaspoon vanilla in saucepan. Cook for 2 minutes; remove from heat. Stir in ½ cup walnuts. Drizzle over warm coffee cake. Serve warm or cooled.

WALNUT SOUR CREAM COFFEE CAKE

Yield:
16 servings
Utensil:
tube pan

Approx Per
Serving:
Cal 234
Prot 3 g
Carbo 29 g
Fiber 1 g
T Fat 12 g
Chol 33 mg
Sod 223 mg

½ cup margarine,
    softened
1 cup sugar
2 eggs
1 cup sour cream
2 cups flour
1 teaspoon baking
    powder

1 teaspoon soda
½ teaspoon salt
1 teaspoon vanilla
    extract
¼ cup sugar
½ teaspoon cinnamon
½ cup chopped
    walnuts

Cream margarine and 1 cup sugar in mixer bowl until light and fluffy. Add eggs and sour cream; beat until smooth. Sift in flour, baking power, soda and salt; mix well. Mix in vanilla; batter will be thin. Mix ¼ cup sugar, cinnamon and walnuts in small bowl. Layer batter and walnut mixture ½ at a time in greased and floured tube pan. Bake at 350 degrees for 45 minutes. Cool in pan for 10 minutes. Remove to wire rack or serving plate.

CONNECTICUT CRULLERS

Yield:
30 servings
Utensil:
deep-fryer

Approx Per Serving:
Cal 131
Prot 2 g
Carbo 24 g
Fiber <1 g
T Fat 3 g
Chol 20 mg
Sod 90 mg

2 tablespoons butter, softened
1 cup sugar
2 eggs, beaten
4 cups flour
3½ teaspoons baking powder
½ teaspoon nutmeg
½ teaspoon salt
1 cup cream
Oil for deep frying
1 cup confectioners' sugar

Cream butter and sugar in mixer bowl until light and fluffy. Beat in eggs. Add flour, baking powder, nutmeg, salt and cream; mix well to form dough. Pat out on lightly floured board. Cut into thin strips. Place 2 strips together and twist to form crullers. Deep-fry in hot oil until golden brown; drain. Coat with confectioners' sugar.

Nutritional information does not include oil for deep frying.

YANKEE SCONES

Yield:
10 servings
Utensil:
baking sheet

Approx Per Serving:
Cal 216
Prot 4 g
Carbo 29 g
Fiber 1 g
T Fat 9 g
Chol 27 mg
Sod 196 mg

2 cups all-purpose flour
4½ teaspoons sugar
½ teaspoon soda
½ teaspoon cream of tartar
½ teaspoon salt
2 tablespoons unsalted butter
¾ to 1 cup buttermilk
¼ cup sugar
3 ounces cream cheese, softened
¼ cup sour cream
7½ teaspoons confectioners' sugar
¼ cup whipping cream

Sift flour, 4½ teaspoons sugar, soda, cream of tartar and salt together in bowl. Cut butter into dry ingredients until crumbly. Stir in enough buttermilk to make medium dough. Knead on floured surface 2 or 3 times. Roll ½ inch thick; cut with 2-inch cutter. Place on baking sheet. Sprinkle with ¼ cup sugar. Bake in preheated 475-degree oven for 15 minutes or until golden brown. Blend cream cheese and sour cream in mixer bowl until light and fluffy. Beat in confectioners' sugar and whipping cream. Serve spread with scones.

Honey Bunnies

4¹/₂ to 5 cups flour
2 envelopes dry yeast
1 teaspoon salt
²/₃ cup evaporated milk
¹/₂ cup water
¹/₂ cup honey

¹/₂ cup margarine
2 eggs, at room
  temperature
¹/₂ cup honey
¹/₄ cup margarine
30 raisins

Mix flour, yeast and salt in bowl. Heat evaporated milk, water, ¹/₂ cup honey and ¹/₂ cup margarine in saucepan until warm; margarine may not melt. Add honey mixture and eggs to dry ingredients gradually. Beat at medium speed for 2 minutes. Stir in any additional flour needed to make stiff dough. Place in bowl sprayed with nonstick cooking spray; spray top of dough. Chill, tightly covered, for 2 to 24 hours. Divide dough into 15 portions. Roll into 20-inch ropes on lightly floured surface. Divide each rope into one 12-inch piece, one 5-inch piece and one 3-inch piece. Coil 12-inch pieces on greased baking sheet to form bunny bodies. Coil 5-inch pieces against body portions to form heads. Shape 3-inch portion into ears and tails; attach to bunnies. Let rise, covered, in warm place for 20 to 25 minutes or until doubled in bulk. Bake at 375 degrees for 12 to 15 minutes or until golden brown. Remove carefully to wire racks. Heat ¹/₂ cup honey with ¹/₄ cup margarine in saucepan over low heat until margarine melts; mix well. Brush over warm bunnies. Place raisins for eyes; brush again with honey glaze. Let stand until cool.

JOHNNY CAKE

Yield:
8 servings
Utensil:
round baking pan

Approx Per
Serving:
Cal 297
Prot 6 g
Carbo 38 g
Fiber 2 g
T Fat 14 g
Chol 62 mg
Sod 478 mg

1¹/₂ cups sifted flour
1 cup yellow cornmeal
¹/₄ cup sugar
1 tablespoon baking
  powder
1 teaspoon soda
¹/₂ teaspoon salt
1 cup milk
¹/₂ cup melted butter
1 egg, slightly beaten

Combine flour, cornmeal, sugar, baking powder, soda, salt, milk, butter and egg in bowl; mix well. Spoon into greased round 9-inch round baking pan. Bake at 400 degrees for 25 minutes.

APPLE CRANBERRY NUT LOAF

Yield:
12 servings
Utensil:
loaf pan

Approx Per
Serving:
Cal 269
Prot 3 g
Carbo 36 g
Fiber 1 g
T Fat 13 g
Chol 19 mg
Sod 257 mg

¹/₂ cup shortening
1 cup sugar
1 egg
¹/₂ cup milk
2 cups flour
1 teaspoon soda
¹/₂ teaspoon cinnamon
1 teaspoon salt
1 cup chopped peeled
  apples
¹/₂ cup chopped fresh
  or frozen cranberries
¹/₂ cup chopped pecans

Cream shortening and sugar in mixer bowl until light and fluffy. Beat in egg and milk. Mix flour, soda, cinnamon and salt in bowl. Stir in apples, cranberries and pecans. Add to creamed mixture; mix with wooden spoon. Spoon into loaf pan sprayed with nonstick cooking spray. Bake at 350 degrees for 1 hour or until loaf tests done. Remove to wire rack to cool. May sprinkle with confectioners' sugar if desired.

APRICOT WALNUT BREAD

Yield:
12 servings
Utensil:
loaf pan

Approx Per
Serving:
Cal 281
Prot 6 g
Carbo 41 g
Fiber 2 g
T Fat 11 g
Chol 22 mg
Sod 357 mg

1 cup quick-cooking
   oats
2 cups baking mix
³/₄ cup sugar
1 teaspoon baking
   powder
¹/₄ teaspoon salt
1 cup chopped dried
   apricots
1 cup chopped walnuts
1 egg
1¹/₄ cups milk

Mix oats, baking mix, sugar, baking powder and salt in bowl. Add apricots and walnuts. Beat egg with milk in small bowl. Add to dry mixture; beat for 30 seconds. Spoon into greased and floured 5x9-inch loaf pan. Bake at 350 degrees for 1 hour. Remove to wire rack to cool.

HOMEMADE BANANA BREAD

Yield:
12 servings
Utensil:
loaf pan

Approx Per
Serving:
Cal 224
Prot 3 g
Carbo 31 g
Fiber 1 g
T Fat 10 g
Chol 36 mg
Sod 183 mg

1³/₄ cups sifted flour
1 tablespoon baking
   powder
²/₃ cup sugar
¹/₂ teaspoon salt
2 eggs, beaten
¹/₂ cup oil
2 or 3 bananas, mashed

Mix flour, baking powder, sugar and salt in bowl. Add eggs, oil and bananas; beat until smooth. Spoon into greased and floured loaf pan. Bake at 350 degrees for 1 hour to 1 hour and 5 minutes or until wooden pick inserted in center comes out clean and top is golden brown. Remove to wire rack to cool. May substitute ¹/₂ cup butter-flavored shortening or chunky peanut butter for oil.

DATE NUT BREAD

1½ cups boiling water
1 8-ounce package
   dates, chopped
1 tablespoon butter
½ cup packed brown
   sugar
½ cup sugar
1 egg
1 teaspoon vanilla
   extract
1½ cups plus 2
   tablespoons flour
2 teaspoons soda
½ teaspoon salt
½ cup chopped
   walnuts

Pour boiling water over dates in bowl. Add butter. Let cool to lukewarm. Combine brown sugar, sugar, egg and vanilla in large bowl; mix well. Mix flour, soda and salt in small bowl. Add dry ingredients to egg mixture alternately with dates, mixing well after each addition. Mix in walnuts. Spoon into greased and floured loaf pan. Bake at 350 degrees for 45 minutes or until wooden pick inserted in center comes out clean. Cool in pan on wire rack. Serve with cream cheese.

IRISH BREAD

2½ cups sifted flour
2 teaspoons baking
   powder
½ teaspoon soda
½ cup sugar
1 teaspoon salt
2 cups sour cream
¼ cup shortening
2 eggs
1 cup raisins
2 teaspoons caraway
   seed

Combine flour, baking powder, soda, sugar, salt, sour cream, shortening and eggs in bowl; mix well. Fold in raisins and caraway seed. Spoon into greased and floured loaf pan. Bake at 350 degrees for 1 hour. Remove to wire rack to cool. May omit caraway seed if preferred.

Irish Soda Bread

Yield:
12 servings
Utensil:
round baking pan

3 cups flour
1/2 cup sugar
1 tablespoon baking
   powder
1/2 cup shortening
1 cup raisins
1 egg
1 cup milk

Approx Per Serving:
Cal 283
Prot 5 g
Carbo 44 g
Fiber 2 g
T Fat 10 g
Chol 21 mg
Sod 99 mg

Mix flour, sugar and baking powder in bowl. Cut in shortening until mixture resembles cornmeal. Add raisins. Beat egg with milk in small bowl. Reserve 1 tablespoon mixture for top. Add remaining egg mixture to dry ingredients; mix well. Pat into greased and lightly floured round 9-inch baking pan. Cut cross in top. Brush with reserved egg mixture. Bake at 375 degrees for 45 minutes to 1 hour or until bread tests done. Serve warm or cool with butter.

Lemon Nut Bread

Yield:
12 servings
Utensil:
loaf pan

1/3 cup oil
1/2 cup sugar
2 eggs
1 1/2 cups flour
1 teaspoon baking
   powder
1/2 teaspoon salt
1/2 cup milk
Grated rind of 1 lemon
Juice of 1 lemon
1/2 cup chopped pecans
1/2 cup sugar

Approx Per Serving:
Cal 228
Prot 3 g
Carbo 30 g
Fiber 1 g
T Fat 11 g
Chol 37 mg
Sod 133 mg

Combine oil, 1/2 cup sugar, eggs, flour, baking powder, salt, milk, lemon rind, half the lemon juice and pecans in bowl; mix well. Spoon into greased and floured loaf pan. Bake at 325 degrees for 45 minutes. Cool in pan for 10 minutes. Combine 1/2 cup sugar and remaining lemon juice in small bowl; mix until sugar dissolves. Spoon over warm cake in pan.

PUMPKIN TEA BREAD

Yield:
24 servings
Utensil:
2 loaf pans

Approx Per
Serving:
Cal 211
Prot 3 g
Carbo 37 g
Fiber 1 g
T Fat 6 g
Chol 18 mg
Sod 216 mg

3⅓ cups flour
½ teaspoon baking
  powder
2 teaspoons soda
1 teaspoon cinnamon
1 teaspoon pumpkin
  pie spice

1½ teaspoons salt
1 16-ounce can
  pumpkin
⅔ cup water
⅔ cup shortening
2⅔ cups sugar
2 eggs

Sift flour, baking powder, soda, cinnamon, pumpkin pie spice and salt together. Mix pumpkin and water in small bowl. Combine shortening, sugar and eggs in large mixer bowl. Beat at high speed for 3 minutes. Add dry ingredients alternately with pumpkin, mixing well after each addition. Spoon into 2 greased and floured 5x9-inch loaf pans. Bake at 350 degrees for 45 minutes or until wooden pick inserted in center comes out clean. Cool in pans for 5 minutes. Remove to wire rack to cool completely.

PUMPKIN LOAF

Yield:
1 serving
Utensil:
loaf pan

Approx Per
Serving:
Cal 429
Prot 25 g
Carbo 60 g
Fiber 2 g
T Fat 11 g
Chol 296 mg
Sod 682 mg

½ cup canned
  pumpkin
1 egg
⅓ cup nonfat dry milk
½ teaspoon soda
3 tablespoons flour
2 tablespoons water
1 teaspoon cinnamon
1 teaspoon pumpkin
  pie spice
½ teaspoon vanilla
  extract

Artificial sweetener to
  equal 8 teaspoons
  sugar
1 tablespoon raisins
¼ cup part-skim milk
  ricotta cheese
¼ cup unsweetened
  crushed pineapple
Artificial sweetener to
  equal 2 teaspoons
  sugar

Combine pumpkin, egg, dry milk, soda, flour, water, cinnamon, pumpkin pie spice, vanilla, artificial sweetener to equal 8 teaspoons sugar and raisins in bowl; mix well. Spoon into miniature loaf pan sprayed with nonstick cooking spray. Bake at 350 degrees for 30 minutes. Remove to serving plate. Combine ricotta cheese, pineapple and artificial sweetener to equal 2 teaspoons sugar in bowl; mix well. Spread on loaf.

PUMPKIN BREAD

Yield:
24 servings
Utensil:
2 loaf pans

Approx Per Serving:
Cal 253
Prot 3 g
Carbo 41 g
Fiber 1 g
T Fat 9 g
Chol 36 mg
Sod 134 mg

3¹/₃ cups flour
¹/₂ teaspoon baking
  powder
2 teaspoons soda
1 teaspoon cinnamon
1 teaspoon cloves
¹/₂ teaspoon salt
²/₃ cup shortening

2²/₃ cups sugar
4 eggs
1 16-ounce can
  pumpkin
²/₃ cup water
²/₃ cup pecans
²/₃ cup raisins

Mix first 6 ingredients together. Cream shortening and sugar in mixer bowl until light and fluffy. Stir in eggs, pumpkin and water. Add dry ingredients; mix well. Fold in pecans and raisins. Spoon into 2 greased and floured loaf pans. Bake at 350 degrees for 1 hour and 5 minutes to 1 hour and 15 minutes or until loaves test done. Remove to wire rack to cool.

HARVEST PUMPKIN LOAF

Yield:
12 servings
Utensil:
loaf pan

Approx Per Serving:
Cal 342
Prot 5 g
Carbo 45 g
Fiber 2 g
T Fat 17 g
Chol 36 mg
Sod 265 mg

1³/₄ cups flour
1 teaspoon soda
1 teaspoon cinnamon
¹/₂ teaspoon ginger
¹/₂ teaspoon nutmeg
¹/₄ teaspoon cloves
¹/₂ teaspoon salt
¹/₂ cup margarine,
  softened
1 cup sugar
2 eggs

³/₄ cup mashed cooked
  pumpkin
³/₄ cup chocolate chips
³/₄ cup chopped
  walnuts
¹/₂ cup confectioners'
  sugar
¹/₈ teaspoon cinnamon
¹/₈ teaspoon nutmeg
1 to 2 tablespoons
  evaporated milk

Sift flour, soda, 1 teaspoon cinnamon, ginger, ¹/₂ teaspoon nutmeg, cloves and salt together. Cream margarine in mixer bowl until light. Add sugar gradually, mixing at low speed until fluffy. Beat in eggs 1 at a time. Add dry ingredients alternately with pumpkin, mixing with spoon after each addition. Stir in chocolate chips and ¹/₂ cup walnuts. Spoon into greased and lightly floured 5x9-inch loaf pan. Sprinkle with remaining ¹/₄ cup walnuts. Bake at 350 degrees for 1 hour and 5 minutes or until bread tests done. Cool in pan for 5 minutes. Remove to wire rack to cool completely. Combine confectioners' sugar, ¹/₈ teaspoon cinnamon and ¹/₈ teaspoon nutmeg in small bowl. Blend in enough evaporated milk to make of desired consistency. Drizzle over loaf.

STRAWBERRY PECAN BREAD

Yield:
12 servings
Utensil:
loaf pan

Approx Per
Serving:
Cal 545
Prot 7 g
Carbo 64 g
Fiber 3 g
T Fat 31 g
Chol 71 mg
Sod 272 mg

4 eggs
1 cup oil
2 cups sugar
2 10-ounce packages
   frozen strawberries,
   thawed

3 cups flour
1 teaspoon soda
1 teaspoon cinnamon
1 teaspoon salt
1½ cups chopped
   pecans

Beat eggs in mixer bowl until thick and lemon-colored. Add oil, sugar and strawberries. Sift in flour, soda, cinnamon and salt; mix well. Stir in pecans. Spoon into greased and floured loaf pan. Bake at 350 degrees for 1 hour and 10 minutes or until loaf tests done. Cool in pan for 10 minutes. Remove to wire rack to cool completely. Chill until serving time.

BASIC YEAST BREAD

Yield:
12 servings
Utensil:
loaf pan

Approx Per
Serving:
Cal 195
Prot 6 g
Carbo 41 g
Fiber 2 g
T Fat 1 g
Chol 0 mg
Sod 534 mg

1 envelope dry yeast
2 cups lukewarm water
1 tablespoon sugar

1 tablespoon salt
4 to 5 cups flour

Dissolve yeast in warm water in large bowl. Add sugar, salt and 1 cup flour; mix well. Add 1½ cups flour; mix well. Add enough remaining flour gradually to form stiff dough, mixing well after each addition. Knead on floured surface for 10 minutes or until smooth and elastic, kneading in additional flour if needed for desired consistency. Shape into loaf; place in greased loaf pan. Let rise, loosely covered with plastic, until doubled in bulk. Bake at 350 degrees for 45 to 55 minutes or until bread sounds hollow when tapped. Remove to wire rack to cool.

BLUEBERRY LEMON MUFFINS

Yield:
12 servings
Utensil:
muffin pan

Approx Per
Serving:
Cal 240
Prot 4 g
Carbo 35 g
Fiber 1 g
T Fat 9 g
Chol 59 mg
Sod 148 mg

2 eggs
1/2 cup melted butter
1 cup sugar
8 ounces plain
    whole-milk yogurt
2 cups flour
1 teaspoon baking
    powder
1/2 teaspoon soda
1 teaspoon lemon rind
1 cup blueberries

Combine eggs, butter and sugar in large mixer bowl; beat until smooth. Stir in yogurt. Add flour, baking powder, soda and lemon rind; mix just until moistened. Fold in blueberries. Spoon into greased muffin cups. Bake at 375 degrees for 25 minutes. May use drained frozen blueberries.

BLUEBERRY MUFFINS

Yield:
42 servings
Utensil:
miniature
muffin pan

Approx Per
Serving:
Cal 132
Prot 2 g
Carbo 19 g
Fiber <1 g
T Fat 6 g
Chol 16 mg
Sod 49 mg

1 cup shortening
2 cups sugar
3 eggs
1 teaspoon vanilla
    extract
2 cups blueberries
3 cups flour
1 tablespoon baking
    powder
1/3 teaspoon salt
1 1/4 cups milk
1/4 cup sugar

Combine shortening, 2 cups sugar, eggs and vanilla in mixer bowl; beat until smooth. Toss blueberries with 1/2 cup flour. Add remaining 2 1/2 cups flour, baking powder, salt and milk to batter; mix well. Fold in blueberries. Spoon into greased miniature muffin cups. Sprinkle with 1/4 cup sugar. Bake at 375 degrees for 30 minutes.

JORDAN MARSH BLUEBERRY MUFFINS

Yield:
12 servings
Utensil:
muffin pan

Approx Per
Serving:
Cal 246
Prot 4 g
Carbo 38 g
Fiber 1 g
T Fat 9 g
Chol 58 mg
Sod 227 mg

2 cups flour
2 teaspoons baking
  powder
1/2 teaspoon salt
1/2 cup butter, softened
1 cup sugar

2 eggs
1/2 cup milk
1 teaspoon vanilla
  extract
2 1/2 cups blueberries

Sift flour, baking powder and salt together. Cream butter and sugar in mixer bowl until light and fluffy. Beat in eggs 1 at a time. Add dry ingredients alternately with milk, mixing well after each addition. Add vanilla. Mash 1/2 cup blueberries. Stir into batter. Fold in remaining 2 cups blueberries. Fill greased muffin cups 3/4 full. Bake at 350 degrees for 30 minutes.

MEME'S BLUEBERRY MUFFINS

Yield:
12 servings
Utensil:
muffin pan

Approx Per
Serving:
Cal 280
Prot 4 g
Carbo 43 g
Fiber 1 g
T Fat 10 g
Chol 38 mg
Sod 198 mg

1/2 cup butter-flavored
  shortening
1 cup sugar
2 eggs, beaten
1 teaspoon vanilla
  extract

2 1/2 cups flour
1 tablespoon baking
  powder
1/2 teaspoon salt
1 cup milk
1 cup blueberry mix

Cream shortening and sugar in mixer bowl until light and fluffy. Beat in eggs and vanilla. Add flour, baking powder and salt; mix well. Add milk and blueberry mix; mix until moistened. Spoon into paper-lined muffin cups. Bake at 350 degrees for 20 minutes or until wooden pick inserted in centers comes out clean.

ICE CREAM MUFFINS

1½ cups flour
1 tablespoon baking powder
1 teaspoon salt
1 egg
2 tablespoons oil
2 cups vanilla ice cream, softened

Mix flour, baking powder and salt in bowl. Add egg, oil and ice cream; mix just until moistened. Fill greased muffin cups ¾ full. Bake at 425 degrees for 20 to 25 minutes or until golden brown. May add ½ cup chocolate chips or sprinkle with cinnamon-sugar if desired.

JOHNNY CAKE CORN MUFFINS

¼ cup margarine, softened
1 cup sugar
1 egg
1 cup milk
1 tablespoon vanilla extract
2 cups flour
1 cup cornmeal
2 teaspoons baking powder
Salt to taste

Combine margarine, sugar, egg, milk and vanilla in mixer bowl; beat until smooth. Add flour, cornmeal, baking powder and salt; mix just until smooth. Spoon into greased muffin cups. Bake at 350 degrees for 30 minutes or until muffins test done. May bake in 9x9-inch baking pan or cornstick pan if preferred.

LEMONY DATE AND PECAN MUFFINS

Yield:
12 servings
Utensil:
muffin pan

*Approx Per
Serving:*
Cal 278
Prot 4 g
Carbo 42 g
Fiber 2 g
T Fat 12 g
Chol 35 mg
Sod 511 mg

1³/₄ cups flour
1¹/₂ teaspoons baking
  powder
1¹/₂ teaspoons soda
1³/₄ teaspoons salt
5 tablespoons butter
¹/₄ cup honey
5 tablespoons lemon
  juice

¹/₂ cup packed brown
  sugar
¹/₂ cup sour cream
1 egg
1 tablespoon grated
  lemon rind
1 cup chopped dates
²/₃ cup chopped pecans

Mix flour, baking powder, soda and salt in bowl. Melt butter with honey in saucepan. Add lemon juice and brown sugar; mix well. Combine sour cream, egg and lemon rind in bowl. Add honey mixture; mix well. Add dry ingredients; mix well. Fold in dates, pecans and enough hot water to make of desired consistency. Fill greased muffin cups ²/₃ full. Bake at 400 degrees for 20 to 25 minutes or until muffins test done.

OAT BRAN MUFFINS

Yield:
12 servings
Utensil:
muffin pan

*Approx Per
Serving:*
Cal 144
Prot 3 g
Carbo 20 g
Fiber 2 g
T Fat 6 g
Chol 21 mg
Sod 208 mg

1¹/₄ cups flour
2 tablespoons sugar
1 tablespoon baking
  powder
¹/₄ teaspoon salt

2 cups Cracklin' Oat
  Bran cereal
1 cup milk
1 egg
3 tablespoons oil

Mix flour, sugar, baking powder and salt together. Combine cereal and milk in bowl. Let stand for 2 minutes. Add egg and oil; mix well. Add dry ingredients; mix just until moistened. Spoon into lightly greased 2¹/₂-inch muffin cups. Bake at 400 degrees for 25 minutes or until light brown. Serve muffins warm.

DESSERTS

Old Man of the Mountain

QUICK APPLE CRISP

Yield:
9 servings
Utensil:
baking dish

*Approx Per
Serving:*
Cal 167
Prot 1 g
Carbo 28 g
Fiber 2 g
T Fat 6 g
Chol 14 mg
Sod 130 mg

5 Granny Smith
  apples, peeled,
  sliced
¼ cup sugar

1 teaspoon cinnamon
½ package Jiffy
  yellow cake mix
¼ cup melted butter

Place apple slices in lightly buttered 9-inch square baking dish. Mix sugar and cinnamon together. Sprinkle over apples. Sprinkle with cake mix. Drizzle with melted butter. Bake at 350 degrees for 30 minutes. Serve warm topped with ice cream.

APPLE SQUARES

Yield:
15 servings
Utensil:
baking dish

*Approx Per
Serving:*
Cal 461
Prot 5 g
Carbo 51 g
Fiber 2 g
T Fat 28 g
Chol 28 mg
Sod 208 mg

2 cups sugar
2 eggs
1½ cups oil
3 cups flour
1 teaspoon soda
1 teaspoon salt

1 teaspoon cinnamon
¼ teaspoon nutmeg
1 cup chopped walnuts
3 cups finely chopped
  apples

Combine sugar, eggs and oil in mixer bowl; mix well. Mix flour, soda, salt, cinnamon and nutmeg together. Add to mixture; beat well. Stir in walnuts and apples. Pour into ungreased 9x13-inch baking dish. Bake at 325 degrees for 1 hour. Cut into squares.

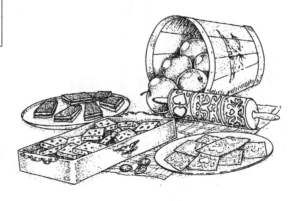

COBBLER

Yield:
16 servings
Utensil:
baking dish

1/2 cup butter
1 cup milk
1 cup flour
1 teaspoon baking
  powder

1 cup sugar
1/2 teaspoon salt
Cinnamon to taste
2 cups sliced apples

*Approx Per
Serving:*
Cal 145
Prot 1 g
Carbo 21 g
Fiber 1 g
T Fat 6 g
Chol 18 mg
Sod 142 mg

Melt butter in 8-inch square baking dish. Combine milk, flour, baking powder, sugar, salt and cinnamon in bowl; mix well. Pour into cake pan. Layer fruit over batter. Bake at 350 degrees for 25 minutes or until crust comes to top and browns. May substitute fruit of your choice for apples.

APPLE BRANDY CHEESECAKE

Yield:
12 servings
Utensil:
springform pan

1¼ cups graham
  cracker crumbs
1/3 cup ground walnuts
1/3 cup melted butter
1/2 teaspoon cinnamon
32 ounces cream
  cheese, softened
1 cup sugar
3 tablespoons apple
  brandy
1 teaspoon cinnamon
1/8 teaspoon nutmeg

1/2 teaspoon vanilla
  extract
4 eggs
1/4 cup whipping cream
1 cup chunk-style
  applesauce
3/4 cup packed brown
  sugar
3/4 cup flour
1/3 cup butter
1/2 teaspoon cinnamon
1/4 teaspoon nutmeg

*Approx Per
Serving:*
Cal 522
Prot 15 g
Carbo 45 g
Fiber 2 g
T Fat 62 g
Chol 257 mg
Sod 530 mg

Combine graham cracker crumbs, walnuts, melted butter and 1/2 teaspoon cinnamon in bowl; mix well. Press into bottom and 1½-inches up side of 9-inch springform pan. Bake at 350 degrees for 10 minutes. Cool to room temperature. Combine cream cheese, sugar and brandy in mixer bowl; beat well. Add 1 teaspoon cinnamon, 1/8 teaspoon nutmeg and vanilla. Beat in eggs 1 at a time. Stir in whipping cream and applesauce. Pour into cooled crust. Bake at 350 degrees for 50 minutes or until center is almost set. Mix brown sugar and flour in bowl. Cut in 1/3 cup butter until crumbly. Stir in 1/2 teaspoon cinnamon and 1/4 teaspoon nutmeg. Sprinkle over cheesecake. Bake for 10 minutes longer or until topping is brown.

BAVARIAN CHEESECAKE

Yield:
12 servings
Utensil:
springform pan

Approx Per Serving:
Cal 485
Prot 8 g
Carbo 31 g
Fiber <1 g
T Fat 38 g
Chol 178 mg
Sod 231 mg

1½ cups graham cracker crumbs
3 tablespoons brown sugar
1 teaspoon cinnamon
6 tablespoons melted butter
24 ounces cream cheese, softened

1½ cups sugar
4 eggs
2 cups sour cream
1 tablespoon flour
1 cup whipping cream
2 tablespoons lemon juice
½ teaspoon vanilla extract

Combine first 4 ingredients in bowl; mix well. Reserve 1 tablespoon mixture for topping. Press remaining mixture into bottom and up sides of buttered 9-inch springform pan. Wrap in foil. Chill until firm. Combine cream cheese and sugar in mixer bowl; beat until well blended and fluffy. Add eggs 1 at a time, beating well after each addition. Add sour cream, flour, whipping cream, lemon juice and vanilla; beat well. Pour into prepared crust. Sprinkle reserved crumbs over top. Bake at 350 degrees for 1 hour. Turn off heat. Let cake stand in closed oven for 1 hour. Cool on wire rack. Remove side of pan.

CHOCOLATE TURTLE CHEESECAKE

Yield:
12 servings
Utensil:
springform pan

Approx Per Serving:
Cal 549
Prot 8 g
Carbo 53 g
Fiber 1 g
T Fat 36 g
Chol 106 mg
Sod 315 mg

2 cups vanilla wafer crumbs
6 tablespoons melted butter
1   14-ounce package caramels
1   5-ounce can evaporated milk
1 cup chopped pecans, toasted

16 ounces cream cheese, softened
½ cup sugar
1 teaspoon vanilla extract
2 eggs
½ cup semisweet chocolate chips, melted

Combine vanilla wafer crumbs and melted butter in bowl; mix well. Press into bottom and up sides of 9-inch springform pan. Bake at 350 degrees for 10 minutes. Melt caramels in evaporated milk in heavy saucepan, stirring frequently. Pour over baked crust. Sprinkle with pecans. Mix cream cheese, sugar and vanilla in mixer bowl. Beat in eggs 1 at a time. Add melted chocolate; mix well. Pour over pecans. Bake at 350 degrees for 10 minutes. Cool in pan for several minutes. Loosen cake from rim of pan. Cool completely; remove rim from pan. Chill in refrigerator.

DIANE'S CHEESECAKE

Yield:
12 servings
Utensil:
springform pan

Approx Per
Serving:
Cal 309
Prot 3 g
Carbo 24 g
Fiber 1 g
T Fat 22 g
Chol 126 mg
Sod 102 mg

2 3-ounce packages ladyfingers
1 pint whipping cream
1 teaspoon sugar
6 teaspoons vanilla extract
8 ounces cream cheese, softened
1 21-ounce can cherry pie filling

Spray 8-inch springform pan with nonstick cooking spray. Line bottom and sides with ladyfingers. Whip cream in bowl until thickened. Add sugar and vanilla; whip until peaks form. Add cream cheese; beat for 1 minute longer. Spread half the mixture over ladyfingers. Add layer of ladyfingers; top with remaining mixture. Pour pie filling on top; spread to cover. Chill for 2 hours before serving.

PINEAPPLE CHEESECAKE SQUARES

Yield:
15 servings
Utensil:
baking dish

Approx Per
Serving:
Cal 443
Prot 6 g
Carbo 44 g
Fiber 1 g
T Fat 28 g
Chol 61 mg
Sod 200 mg

2/3 cup margarine
2 cups flour
1/2 cup confectioners' sugar
1/2 cup finely chopped almonds
16 ounces cream cheese, softened
1/2 cup sugar
2 eggs
2/3 cup unsweetened pineapple juice
1/4 cup flour
1/4 cup sugar
1 20-ounce can crushed pineapple
12 ounces whipped topping

Cut margarine into 2 cups flour and confectioners' sugar until crumbly. Stir in almonds. Press into 9x13-inch baking dish. Bake at 350 degrees for 15 to 20 minutes. Combine cream cheese and 1/2 cup sugar in mixer bowl; mix well. Add eggs 1 at a time, beating well after each addition. Add pineapple juice; mix well. Pour into hot crust. Bake at 350 degrees for 20 minutes or until center is set. Cool to room temperature. Combine 1/4 cup flour and 1/4 cup sugar in saucepan; mix well. Drain pineapple, reserving 1 cup juice. Add juice to saucepan; mix well. Cook for 1 minute or until thickened, stirring constantly. Remove from heat. Stir in pineapple. Cool to room temperature. Fold whipped topping into cooled pineapple mixture. Spread over cheesecake. Chill for 4 hours or until firm. Cut into squares.

Pumpkin Cheesecake

Yield:
12 servings
Utensil:
springform pan

Approx Per Serving:
Cal 434
Prot 7 g
Carbo 46 g
Fiber 1 g
T Fat 26 g
Chol 108 mg
Sod 268 mg

1¼ cups crushed graham crackers
⅓ cup melted butter
1 16-ounce can juice-pack crushed pineapple
1 16-ounce can pumpkin
1 cup packed brown sugar
3 eggs, beaten
1 teaspoon cinnamon
½ teaspoon ginger
1 envelope unflavored gelatin
16 ounces cream cheese, softened
1 tablespoon vanilla extract
1 cup miniature marshmallows
8 ounces whipped topping

Mix graham cracker crumbs and melted butter in bowl. Press into bottom and 1½ to 2 inches up side of 9-inch springform pan. Bake at 350 degrees for 10 minutes. Cool to room temperature. Drain pineapple well, reserving ¾ cup juice. Chill pineapple, covered, in refrigerator. Combine pineapple juice and next 6 ingredients in saucepan; mix well. Simmer, covered, for 30 minutes, stirring occasionally. Beat cream cheese and vanilla in mixer bowl until fluffy. Beat in pumpkin mixture gradually. Pour into graham cracker crust. Chill, covered, in refrigerator. Fold pineapple and marshmallows into whipped topping in bowl. Spread over cheesecake. Chill until serving time. Remove sides from springform pan.

Banana-Strawberry Trifle

Yield:
8 servings
Utensil:
serving bowl

Approx Per Serving:
Cal 567
Prot 9 g
Carbo 77 g
Fiber 3 g
T Fat 25 g
Chol 77 mg
Sod 438 mg

1 16-ounce pound cake, cut into cubes
2 4-ounce packages banana instant pudding mix
4 cups milk
2 10-ounce packages frozen strawberries, thawed
12 ounces whipped topping

Place pound cake cubes in serving bowl. Combine instant pudding mix and milk in mixer bowl; beat well. Pour over pound cake. Spoon strawberries over pudding. Chill until serving time. Top with whipped topping.

CHERRY CHOCOLATE CHIP ICE CREAM

Yield:
18 servings
Utensil:
ice cream freezer

**Approx Per
Serving:**
*Cal 383
Prot 6 g
Carbo 55 g
Fiber 1 g
T Fat 17 g
Chol 120 mg
Sod 158 mg*

2 cups sugar
8 eggs, beaten
2 4-ounce packages
   vanilla instant
   pudding mix
1 quart half and half

1 tablespoon vanilla
   extract
1 cup maraschino
   cherries, chopped
1 16-ounce Hershey
   bar, shaved

Combine sugar, eggs, vanilla pudding mix, half and half and vanilla in mixer bowl; mix well. Pour into ice cream freezer container. Freeze using manufacturer's instructions until thickened. Add chopped cherries and shaved chocolate. Freeze until firm. Store in freezer, adding salt and ice as needed, for 2 to 3 hours before serving.

PRETZEL SALAD DESSERT

Yield:
15 servings
Utensil:
baking dish

**Approx Per
Serving:**
*Cal 353
Prot 3 g
Carbo 41 g
Fiber 1 g
T Fat 20 g
Chol 17 mg
Sod 317 mg*

2 cups crushed pretzels
3 tablespoons sugar
3/4 cup melted
   margarine
8 ounces cream cheese,
   softened
1 cup sugar

12 ounces whipped
   topping
2 3-ounce packages
   strawberry gelatin
2 cups boiling water
2 10-ounce packages
   frozen strawberries

Combine pretzels, 3 tablespoons sugar and melted margarine in bowl; mix well. Press into 9x12-inch baking dish. Bake at 400 degrees for 3 to 5 minutes. Cool to room temperature. Combine cream cheese and 1 cup sugar in mixer bowl; mix well. Fold in whipped topping. Spread over cooled crust. Chill in refrigerator. Dissolve gelatin in 2 cups boiling water in bowl. Add frozen strawberries, stirring until strawberries are thawed and mixture thickens. Pour over cream cheese layer. Chill for several hours to overnight.

CINNAMON BREAD PUDDING

Yield:
6 servings
Utensil:
casserole

**Approx Per
Serving:**
Cal 322
Prot 12 g
Carbo 47 g
Fiber 2 g
T Fat 12 g
Chol 103 mg
Sod 373 mg

4 cups milk, scalded
2 cups crumbled bread
 slices
6 tablespoons sugar
2 eggs, beaten
1/2 teaspoon salt

2 teaspoons vanilla
 extract
1 teaspoon cinnamon
1/4 teaspoon nutmeg
1 cup raisins
2 tablespoons butter

Combine scalded milk, bread and sugar in mixer bowl; mix well. Add eggs 1 at a time, beating well after each addition. Add salt, vanilla, cinnamon and nutmeg; mix well. Stir in raisins. Spoon into buttered casserole. Dot with butter. Place casserole in slightly larger pan half filled with hot water. Bake at 375 degrees for 1 hour or until set.

OLD-FASHIONED BREAD PUDDING

Yield:
6 servings
Utensil:
casserole

**Approx Per
Serving:**
Cal 340
Prot 13 g
Carbo 45 g
Fiber <1 g
T Fat 12 g
Chol 203 mg
Sod 275 mg

4 cups milk, scalded
4 to 5 slices bread,
 cubed
3/4 tablespoon butter

3/4 cup sugar
5 eggs, beaten
1 teaspoon vanilla
 extract

Pour scalded milk over cubed bread and butter in bowl. Let stand for 5 minutes. Add sugar, eggs and vanilla; mix well. Pour into greased casserole. Bake at 350 degrees for 1 hour. Place in slightly larger pan half filled with hot water. Let stand until cooled to room temperature.

RICH BREAD PUDDING

Yield:
12 servings
Utensil:
baking dish

Approx Per Serving:
Cal 348
Prot 8 g
Carbo 39 g
Fiber 1 g
T Fat 19 g
Chol 123 mg
Sod 450 mg

1¹/₂ quarts milk, scalded
³/₄ cup margarine
1 cup sugar
6 eggs, beaten

1 teaspoon salt
2 teaspoons cinnamon
4 cups cubed bread
1 cup raisins

Combine scalded milk and margarine in bowl, stirring until margarine is melted. Combine sugar and eggs in mixer bowl; beat well. Add salt and cinnamon; mix well. Add hot milk mixture gradually, beating well. Spread bread cubes in greased 9x13-inch baking dish. Sprinkle with raisins. Pour in mixture. Place baking dish in slightly larger pan half filled with hot water. Bake at 350 degrees for 45 minutes.

GRAPENUT PUDDING

Yield:
6 servings
Utensil:
saucepan

Approx Per Serving:
Cal 554
Prot 11 g
Carbo 55 g
Fiber 2 g
T Fat 34 g
Chol 139 mg
Sod 368 mg

4 cups milk
2 cups grapenuts cereal
¹/₂ cup sugar

2 egg yolks, beaten
2 egg whites, stiffly beaten

Combine milk, cereal, sugar and egg yolks in saucepan; mix well. Heat just to the boiling point, stirring occasionally. Cool to room temperature. Fold in stiffly beaten egg whites. Spoon into serving bowl.

CREAMY NO-BAKE RICE PUDDING

<table>
<tr><td>

Yield:
6 servings
Utensil:
saucepan

</td><td>

1 quart milk
1/4 teaspoon salt
1/2 cup uncooked rice
1/2 cup raisins
1/4 cup evaporated milk

</td><td>

2 eggs, beaten
1/3 cup sugar
1 teaspoon vanilla
   extract
3/4 cup evaporated milk

</td></tr>
</table>

Approx Per
Serving:
Cal 322
Prot 12 g
Carbo 46 g
Fiber 1 g
T Fat 11 g
Chol 105 mg
Sod 227 mg

Heat milk and salt in heavy saucepan. Stir in rice. Simmer, covered, for 15 to 20 minutes or until rice is tender, stirring occasionally. Stir in raisins and 1/4 cup evaporated milk. Simmer for several minutes longer. Combine eggs, sugar, vanilla and remaining 3/4 cup evaporated milk in bowl; mix well. Stir a small amount of hot rice mixture into egg mixture. Stir egg mixture into hot rice mixture. Pour into serving bowl. Cool slightly, stirring occasionally. Garnish with a sprinkle of nutmeg or cinnamon.

STRAWBERRY ROYALE

Yield:
6 servings
Utensil:
serving bowl

1   10-ounce package
   frozen raspberries
1 quart strawberries,
   sliced

1/4 cup Kirsch liqueur
1 cup whipping cream

Approx Per
Serving:
Cal 254
Prot 2 g
Carbo 26 g
Fiber 5 g
T Fat 15 g
Chol 54 mg
Sod 18 mg

Thaw raspberries, reserving liquid. Purée in blender container. Combine strawberries and liqueur in serving bowl; toss lightly. Add raspberry purée to strawberries; toss lightly. Chill for 2 hours or longer. Serve with cream or whipped cream.

ITALIAN STRAWBERRY SHORTCAKE

Yield:
12 servings
Utensil:
serving bowl

Approx Per
Serving:
Cal 176
Prot 2 g
Carbo 21 g
Fiber 1 g
T Fat 8 g
Chol 51 mg
Sod 24 mg

2 pints strawberries
4 teaspoons sugar
2 3-ounce packages
   ladyfingers, split
   lengthwise

¼ cup dark rum
12 ounces whipped
   topping
¼ cup sweet Marsala
   wine

Reserve 6 strawberries for garnish. Slice remaining berries into mixer bowl. Add sugar; toss gently to mix. Let stand for 20 minutes. Arrange ladyfingers over bottom and around side of large round serving bowl. Sprinkle with rum. Layer half the strawberries, half the whipped topping, all the wine, remaining strawberries and remaining whipped topping over ladyfingers. Garnish with reserved whole strawberries. Chill, covered, for several hours or until serving time.

STRAWBERRY SHORTCAKE

Yield:
12 servings
Utensil:
glass dish

Approx Per
Serving:
Cal 167
Prot 3 g
Carbo 40 g
Fiber 1 g
T Fat <1 g
Chol 0 mg
Sod 204 mg

1 6-ounce package
   strawberry gelatin
2 cups boiling water
2 cups cold water

1 21-ounce can
   strawberry pie filling
1 12-ounce angel food
   cake, cut into cubes

Dissolve gelatin in boiling water in bowl. Stir in cold water. Stir in strawberry pie filling. Sprinkle cake cubes in 9x13-inch glass dish. Pour in strawberry mixture. Chill in refrigerator for 3 hours or longer. Cut into squares. Garnish each serving with whipped cream.

STRAWBERRY SQUARES

½ cup shortening
½ cup sugar
1 egg
½ teaspoon almond
  extract
½ teaspoon salt

1½ cups sifted
  enriched flour
½ teaspoon baking
  powder
¾ cup strawberry
  preserves

Cream shortening and sugar in mixer bowl until light and fluffy. Add egg and almond extract; mix well. Mix salt, flour and baking powder together. Add to mixture; mix well. Spread half the dough in greased 8-inch baking dish. Spread strawberry preserves over dough. Spread remaining dough in waxed paper-lined 8-inch baking dish. Invert onto strawberry preserves, lifting out dough. Remove waxed paper. Bake at 400 degrees for 25 to 30 minutes or until brown. Cool slightly. Cut into 2-inch squares.

STRUDEL

2 cups flour
1 cup margarine,
  softened
1 cup sour cream
1 16-ounce jar apricot
  preserves

½ cup raisins
1 cup chopped walnuts
1 cup confectioners'
  sugar

Combine flour, margarine and sour cream in bowl; mix well. Shape into ball; dust with additional flour. Chill, sealed in plastic bag, overnight. Divide dough into 3 portions. Roll each portion into rectangle on floured surface. Spread apricot preserves over ¾ of the dough; sprinkle raisins and walnuts over preserves. Roll as for jelly roll. Place on baking sheet. Bake at 350 degrees for 40 to 45 minutes or until brown. Cool in pan for several minutes. Cut into diagonal slices; sprinkle with confectioners' sugar.

COOKIES
AND CANDIES

Maple Sugaring in New England

APPLE CHEESE BARS

Yield:
36 servings
Utensil:
baking pan

Approx Per
Serving:
Cal 168
Prot 3 g
Carbo 20 g
Fiber 1 g
T Fat 9 g
Chol 36 mg
Sod 134 mg

½ cup sugar
1 cup butter, softened
2 egg yolks
2 cups flour
1 teaspoon baking
   powder
½ teaspoon salt
4 medium cooking
   apples, peeled

8 ounces Cheddar cheese
¼ cup flour
¾ cup sugar
1 teaspoon cinnamon
2 egg whites
1½ cups
   confectioners' sugar
4 ounces cream cheese,
   softened

Combine ½ cup sugar, butter, egg yolks, 2 cups flour, baking powder and salt in bowl; mix until crumbly. Press half the mixture into 9x13-inch baking pan. Grate apples and cheese by hand or in food processor. Combine with ¼ cup flour, ¾ cup sugar and cinnamon in bowl; mix well. Spread over crust. Sprinkle with remaining crumb mixture. Beat egg whites in mixer bowl until stiff peaks form. Add confectioners' sugar and cream cheese gradually, beating constantly. Spread evenly over layers. Bake at 350 degrees for 30 to 35 minutes or until light golden brown. Cool on wire rack. Cut into bars. May substitute oats for part of flour in crust mixture.

FRENCH APPLE SQUARES

Yield:
48 servings
Utensil:
baking pan

Approx Per
Serving:
Cal 79
Prot 1 g
Carbo 9 g
Fiber <1 g
T Fat 5 g
Chol 5 mg
Sod 51 mg

2½ cups flour
2 tablespoons sugar
1 teaspoon salt
1 cup shortening
1 egg yolk

⅔ cup milk
1   21-ounce can apple
   pie filling
1 egg white

Mix flour, sugar, salt and shortening in bowl until crumbly. Add egg yolk and milk; mix well. Divide into 2 portions. Roll 1 portion on floured surface to fit 10x15-inch baking pan. Spread with apple pie filling. Top with rolled remaining pastry. Brush with egg white. Bake at 375 degrees for 35 minutes. Cool on wire rack. Cut into squares.

APPLE SQUARES

Yield:
24 servings
Utensil:
baking pan

Approx Per Serving:
Cal 290
Prot 3 g
Carbo 32 g
Fiber 1 g
T Fat 17 g
Chol 18 mg
Sod 130 mg

2 cups sugar
2 eggs
1¹/₂ cups oil
3 cups flour
1 teaspoon soda

1 teaspoon cinnamon
¹/₄ teaspoon nutmeg
1 teaspoon salt
1 cup chopped walnuts
3 cups sliced apples

Combine sugar, eggs and oil in bowl; mix well. Stir in flour, soda, cinnamon, nutmeg and salt. Mix in walnuts and apples. Spoon into ungreased 9x13-inch baking pan. Bake at 325 degrees for 1 hour. Cool on wire rack. Cut into squares. May bake in two 8x8-inch baking pans if preferred.

YOGURT APPLE SQUARES

Yield:
24 servings
Utensil:
baking pan

Approx Per Serving:
Cal 188
Prot 2 g
Carbo 29 g
Fiber 1 g
T Fat 8 g
Chol 20 mg
Sod 129 mg

2 cups flour
2 cups packed light
   brown sugar
¹/₂ cup butter, softened
1 cup chopped pecans
2 teaspoons cinnamon
1 teaspoon vanilla
   extract

¹/₂ teaspoon salt
1 teaspoon soda
1 cup plain yogurt
1 egg
2 cups finely chopped
   apples

Combine flour, brown sugar and butter in mixer bowl; mix at medium speed until crumbly. Stir in pecans. Press 2³/₄ cups of the mixture into ungreased 9x13-inch baking pan. Combine crumb mixture with cinnamon, vanilla, salt, soda, yogurt and egg in bowl. Stir in apples. Spoon evenly over crust. Bake at 350 degrees for 40 minutes. Cool to room temperature. Chill in refrigerator for 1 hour. Cut into squares.

Applesauce Bars

½ cup margarine, softened
1 cup sugar
1 egg
1 teaspoon vanilla extract
2 teaspoons soda
1½ cups applesauce
¼ teaspoon cloves
2 cups flour
1 cup raisins
½ teaspoon cinnamon
⅔ cup chopped walnuts

Cream margarine and sugar in mixer bowl until light and fluffy. Blend in egg and vanilla. Dissolve soda in applesauce in small bowl. Stir in cloves. Add to creamed mixture; mix well. Fold in flour, raisins, cinnamon and walnuts. Spoon into greased 10x10-inch baking dish. Bake at 350 degrees for 35 minutes. Cool on wire rack. Cut into bars.

Apricot Date Bars

½ cup butter
½ cup graham cracker crumbs
1 8-ounce package dates, chopped
1 4¾-ounce jar baby food apricots
1 14-ounce can sweetened condensed milk
1 3-ounce can flaked coconut
½ cup coarsely chopped walnuts

Melt butter in 9x13-inch baking pan. Add cracker crumbs; mix well, spreading evenly in pan. Combine dates with apricots in bowl; mix well. Spread evenly over crumbs. Drizzle with condensed milk. Top with coconut and walnuts; press down gently. Bake at 350 degrees for 30 minutes or until light brown. Cool to room temperature. Cut into bars.

APRICOT OATMEAL BARS

Yield:
36 servings
Utensil:
baking pan

Approx Per
Serving:
Cal 102
Prot 1 g
Carbo 15 g
Fiber 1 g
T Fat 4 g
Chol 10 mg
Sod 60 mg

1¼ cups flour
1¼ cups
  quick-cooking oats
½ cup sugar
¾ cup melted butter
½ teaspoon soda
¼ teaspoon salt
2 teaspoons vanilla
  extract
1 12-ounce jar apricot
  preserves
½ cup flaked coconut

Combine flour, oats, sugar, butter, soda, salt and vanilla in 3-quart mixer bowl. Beat at low speed for 2 minutes or until crumbly, scraping side of bowl often. Reserve 1 cup crumbs. Press remaining crumbs into greased 9x13-inch baking pan. Spread apricot preserves over crumbs, spreading to within ½ inch of edges. Combine reserved crumbs with coconut in bowl. Sprinkle over apricots. Bake at 350 degrees for 22 to 27 minutes or until edges are light brown. Cool to room temperature. Cut into bars.

APRICOT BARS

Yield:
36 servings
Utensil:
baking pan

Approx Per
Serving:
Cal 106
Prot 1 g
Carbo 17 g
Fiber <1 g
T Fat 4 g
Chol 10 mg
Sod 23 mg

½ cup unsalted butter,
  softened
⅓ cup packed brown
  sugar
1¼ cups flour
¾ cup apricot
  preserves
¼ cup butter, softened
½ cup packed brown
  sugar
½ teaspoon almond
  extract
¾ cup flour
⅛ teaspoon salt
¾ cup confectioners'
  sugar
1 tablespoon milk
1 tablespoon almond
  extract

Mix ½ cup unsalted butter, ⅓ cup brown sugar and 1¼ cups flour in bowl until crumbly. Press into greased 9x9-inch baking pan. Bake at 350 degrees for 15 to 20 minutes or until light brown. Cool slightly. Spread preserves over crust, leaving ½-inch edge. Cream ¼ cup butter, ½ cup brown sugar and ½ teaspoon almond extract in mixer bowl until light and fluffy. Add ¾ cup flour and salt; mix until crumbly. Sprinkle over preserves. Bake at 350 degrees for 20 to 25 minutes or until light brown. Cool to room temperature. Beat confectioners' sugar, milk and 1 tablespoon almond extract in small bowl until smooth. Drizzle over cooled baked layer. Cut into bars.

BLUEBERRY-RICOTTA SQUARES

Yield:
16 servings
Utensil:
baking pan

Approx Per Serving:
Cal 151
Prot 3 g
Carbo 22 g
Fiber 1 g
T Fat 6 g
Chol 45 mg
Sod 83 mg

1 cup flour
3/4 cup sugar
1 1/4 teaspoons baking powder
1/4 teaspoon salt
1/3 cup milk
1/4 cup shortening
1/2 teaspoon vanilla extract

1 egg
1 1/2 cups fresh or frozen blueberries
1 1/4 cups ricotta cheese
2 eggs
1/3 cup sugar
1/4 teaspoon vanilla extract

Mix flour, 3/4 cup sugar, baking powder and salt in small bowl. Add milk, shortening, 1/2 teaspoon vanilla and egg. Beat at low speed for 2 minutes. Spoon into greased 9x9-inch baking pan. Sprinkle with blueberries. Combine ricotta cheese, 2 eggs, 1/3 cup sugar and 1/4 teaspoon vanilla in medium bowl; beat until smooth. Spread evenly over blueberries. Bake at 350 degrees for 55 to 60 minutes or until knife inserted near center comes out clean. Cool on wire rack. Cut into squares.

BROWNIES

Yield:
16 servings
Utensil:
baking pan

Approx Per Serving:
Cal 164
Prot 2 g
Carbo 19 g
Fiber 1 g
T Fat 10 g
Chol 27 mg
Sod 122 mg

1/3 cup margarine, softened
3/4 cup sugar
1/4 cup corn syrup
2 teaspoons vanilla extract

2 eggs
1/2 cup flour
1/3 cup baking cocoa
1/2 teaspoon salt
1 cup chopped pecans

Cream margarine and sugar in mixer bowl until light and fluffy. Blend in corn syrup and vanilla. Beat in eggs. Add flour, cocoa, salt and pecans; mix well. Spoon into greased 9x9-inch baking pan. Bake at 350 degrees for 25 to 30 minutes or until brownies test done.

PRINCESS BROWNIES

Yield:
24 servings
Utensil:
baking pan

Approx Per
Serving:
Cal 153
Prot 2 g
Carbo 20 g
Fiber <1 g
T Fat 8 g
Chol 33 mg
Sod 90 mg

1 22-ounce package
   brownie mix
8 ounces cream cheese,
   softened
1/2 cup sugar
1 egg
1/2 teaspoon vanilla
   extract

Prepare brownie mix using package directions. Combine cream cheese and sugar in mixer bowl; beat until smooth. Blend in egg and vanilla. Layer half the brownie batter, cream cheese mixture and remaining brownie batter in greased 9x13-inch baking pan. Cut through with knife to marbleize. Bake at 350 degrees for 35 to 40 minutes or until brownies test done. Cool to room temperature. Cut into squares.

RASPBERRY BROWNIES

Yield:
16 servings
Utensil:
baking pan

Approx Per
Serving:
Cal 350
Prot 5 g
Carbo 43 g
Fiber 2 g
T Fat 20 g
Chol 44 mg
Sod 63 mg

3 1-ounce squares
   unsweetened
   chocolate
1/2 cup shortening
3 eggs
1 1/2 cups sugar
1 1/2 teaspoons vanilla
   extract
1/4 teaspoon salt
1 cup flour
1 1/2 cups chopped
   walnuts
1/3 cup raspberry jam
1 1-ounce square
   unsweetened
   chocolate, melted
2 tablespoons butter
2 tablespoons light
   corn syrup
1 cup confectioners'
   sugar
1 tablespoon milk
1 teaspoon vanilla
   extract

Melt 3 squares chocolate with shortening in double boiler over warm water; mix well. Cool slightly. Blend eggs, sugar, 1 1/2 teaspoons vanilla and salt in mixer bowl. Stir in chocolate mixture. Add flour; mix well. Fold in walnuts. Spoon into greased 8x8-inch baking pan. Bake at 325 degrees for 40 minutes. Spread jam over hot brownies. Blend melted chocolate with butter and corn syrup in bowl. Add confectioners' sugar, milk and 1 teaspoon vanilla; mix until smooth. Spread over jam. Garnish with additional walnuts dipped in melted chocolate.

TRI-LEVEL BROWNIES

1 cup quick-cooking oats
1/2 cup flour
1/2 cup packed brown sugar
1/4 teaspoon soda
1/2 teaspoon salt
6 tablespoons melted butter
3/4 cup sugar
1/4 cup melted butter
1 1-ounce square unsweetened chocolate, melted
1 egg
2/3 cup flour
1/4 teaspoon baking powder
1/4 teaspoon salt
1/4 cup milk
1/2 teaspoon vanilla extract
1/2 cup chopped walnuts
1 1-ounce square unsweetened chocolate
2 tablespoons butter
1/2 cup sifted confectioners' sugar
1 teaspoon vanilla extract
2 tablespoons hot water

Mix oats, 1/2 cup flour, brown sugar, soda and 1/2 teaspoon salt in bowl. Add 6 tablespoons melted butter; mix until crumbly. Pat into 7x11-inch baking pan. Bake at 350 degrees for 10 minutes. Combine sugar, 1/4 cup butter, and 1 square melted chocolate in bowl; mix well. Blend in egg. Sift 2/3 cup flour, baking powder and 1/4 teaspoon salt together. Add to chocolate mixture alternately with mixture of milk and 1/2 teaspoon vanilla, mixing well after addition. Fold in walnuts. Spread over baked layer. Bake at 350 degrees for 25 minutes. Cool on wire rack. Melt 1 square chocolate with 2 tablespoons butter in small saucepan over low heat, stirring to mix well; remove from heat. Add confectioners' sugar and 1 teaspoon vanilla; mix well. Blend in enough hot water to make of desired consistency; frosting should be thin. Pour over top of brownies. Cut into squares. Garnish with walnut halves.

Two-Way Brownies

Yield:
24 servings
Utensil:
baking pan

*Approx Per
Serving:*
Cal 244
Prot 3 g
Carbo 29 g
Fiber 1 g
T Fat 14 g
Chol 56 mg
Sod 122 mg

2 cups flour
1/2 teaspoon salt
1 cup butter, softened
2 cups sugar
4 eggs
1/2 teaspoon vanilla
  extract

2 1-ounce squares
   unsweetened
   chocolate, melted
3/4 cup chopped pecans
3/4 cup chocolate chips

Sift flour and salt together. Beat butter, sugar and eggs in mixer bowl until smooth. Add flour mixture; mix well. Mix in vanilla. Divide into 2 portions. Add chocolate and pecans to 1 portion; mix well. Spread in greased 9x13-inch baking pan. Add chocolate chips to second portion. Spread evenly over first layer. Bake at 350 degrees for 30 minutes. Cool on wire rack. Cut into squares.

Chocolate Walnut Bars

Yield:
48 servings
Utensil:
baking pan

*Approx Per
Serving:*
Cal 187
Prot 2 g
Carbo 25 g
Fiber 1 g
T Fat 9 g
Chol 18 mg
Sod 67 mg

3 cups flour
1/2 cup sugar
1/4 teaspoon salt
1 cup margarine,
  softened
6 ounces semisweet
  chocolate

1 1/2 cups corn syrup
1 1/2 cups sugar
4 eggs, beaten
1 1/2 teaspoons vanilla
  extract
2 1/2 cups chopped
  walnuts

Combine flour, 1/2 cup sugar, salt and margarine in mixer bowl; mix until crumbly. Press firmly into greased 10x15-inch baking pan. Bake at 350 degrees for 20 minutes. Melt chocolate with corn syrup in 3 quart saucepan over low heat, stirring to mix well; remove from heat. Stir in 1 1/2 cups sugar, eggs and vanilla. Fold in walnuts. Spoon evenly over crust. Bake for 30 minutes or until firm around edges and slightly soft in center. Cool on wire rack. Cut into bars or squares.

CHOCOLATE POTATO CHIP COOKIES

Yield:
108 servings
Utensil:
cookie sheet

Approx Per
Serving:
Cal 58
Prot 1 g
Carbo 7 g
Fiber <1 g
T Fat 3 g
Chol 4 mg
Sod 32 mg

2 cups flour
1 teaspoon soda
1 cup margarine,
  softened
1 cup sugar
1 cup packed brown
  sugar
2 eggs

1 teaspoon vanilla
  extract
1 cup chopped pecans
6 ounces chocolate
  chips
2 cups crushed potato
  chips

Mix flour and soda together. Cream margarine in mixer bowl until light. Add sugar and brown sugar gradually, beating until fluffy. Add eggs and vanilla; mix well. Stir in flour mixture until smooth. Fold in pecans, chocolate chips and potato chips. Drop by tablespoonfuls onto ungreased cookie sheet. Bake at 350 degrees for 10 to 12 minutes or until golden brown. Remove to wire rack to cool. May chill dough for 1 hour for thicker cookies.

FESTIVE COCONUT MACAROONS

Yield:
30 servings
Utensil:
cookie sheet

Nutritional
information for
this recipe
is not
available.

1 package dry sugar
  cookie mix
1 egg white
1 teaspoon coconut or
  almond extract

1/2 cup coconut
1 egg white
1 1/4 cups coconut
15 candied cherries,
  cut into halves

Combine cookie mix, 1 egg white and coconut extract in bowl; mix well. Stir in 1/2 cup coconut. Shape into 1-inch balls. Dip into remaining egg white; coat with remaining 1 1/4 cups coconut. Place on ungreased cookie sheet. Press 1 candied cherry half into center of each cookie. Bake at 325 degrees for 8 minutes or until coconut is light brown. Cool on cookie sheet for 1 minute. Remove to wire rack to cool completely.

COCONUT SQUARES

Yield:
16 servings
Utensil:
glass dish

Approx Per
Serving:
Cal 199
Prot 2 g
Carbo 22 g
Fiber 1 g
T Fat 13 g
Chol 12 mg
Sod 89 mg

¼ cup butter
1 cup graham cracker
  crumbs
1 teaspoon sugar
1 cup flaked coconut

½ cup chopped pecans
⅔ cup sweetened
  condensed milk
1 cup semisweet
  chocolate chips

Place butter in 9-inch glass dish. Microwave on High for 1 minute or until melted. Add cracker crumbs and sugar; mix well. Press evenly over bottom of dish. Microwave on High for 2 minutes. Cool slightly. Combine coconut, pecans and condensed milk in bowl; mix well. Spoon evenly over crust. Microwave on High for 4 minutes, turning dish ½ turn once. Sprinkle with chocolate chips. Microwave on High for 1 minute. Spread chocolate evenly over top. Cool to room temperature. Cut into squares.

CONGO BARS

Yield:
24 servings
Utensil:
baking pan

Approx Per
Serving:
Cal 238
Prot 3 g
Carbo 32 g
Fiber 1 g
T Fat 12 g
Chol 27 mg
Sod 154 mg

⅔ cup margarine
¼ cup sugar
¾ 1-pound package
  brown sugar
3 eggs
1 teaspoon vanilla
  extract

2½ teaspoons baking
  powder
½ teaspoon salt
2¾ cups flour
1 cup chocolate chips
1 cup chopped pecans

Melt margarine in medium saucepan over medium heat; remove from heat. Stir in sugar and brown sugar. Blend in eggs 1 at a time. Add vanilla, baking powder, salt and 1 cup flour; mix well. Add remaining 1¾ cups flour; mix well. Fold in chocolate and pecans. Spread in greased 9x13-inch baking pan. Bake at 350 degrees for 35 minutes or until layer tests done; do not overbake. Cool on wire rack. Cut into bars.

CRESCENTS

Yield:
36 servings
Utensil:
cookie sheet

Approx Per Serving:
Cal 61
Prot 1 g
Carbo 4 g
Fiber <1 g
T Fat 5 g
Chol 16 mg
Sod 46 mg

1 cup butter
2 cups (or more) flour
1 egg yolk
1/4 teaspoon salt
2/3 cup sour cream

1/2 cup sugar
1 tablespoon cinnamon
1 cup chopped pecans
1 egg white

Cut butter into flour in bowl until crumbly. Add egg yolk and salt; mix well. Add sour cream, mixing to form ball and adding additional flour if needed for handling. Divide into 3 portions. Shape into 3 balls; wrap well. Chill overnight. Roll 1 portion at a time as thin as possible on floured surface. Cut into wedges. Mix sugar, cinnamon and pecans in bowl. Sprinkle over wedges. Roll dough from wide end to enclose filling. Place on cookie sheet, shaping into crescents. Brush with egg white. Bake at 375 degrees for 20 to 25 minutes or until golden brown. Remove to wire rack to cool.

DATE CRUMBLES

Yield:
24 servings
Utensil:
baking pan

Approx Per Serving:
Cal 369
Prot 4 g
Carbo 57 g
Fiber 3 g
T Fat 15 g
Chol 31 mg
Sod 175 mg

16 ounces dates, finely chopped
1 cup chopped walnuts
1 cup sugar
1 1/3 cups water
3 cups flour

2 teaspoons soda
2 cups quick-cooking oats
2 cups packed light brown sugar
1 1/2 cups melted butter

Combine dates, walnuts, sugar and water in saucepan. Cook over medium-high heat until thickened, stirring frequently. Combine flour, soda, oats, brown sugar and butter in bowl; mix until crumbly. Press half the oats mixture into 9x13-inch baking pan. Top with date mixture and remaining oats mixture; press lightly. Bake at 350 degrees for 25 to 30 minutes or until golden brown. Cool on wire rack. Cut into squares.

FILLED DEVIL DOGS

Yield:
18 servings
Utensil:
cookie sheet

Approx Per
Serving:
Cal 153
Prot 3 g
Carbo 24 g
Fiber 1 g
T Fat 6 g
Chol 14 mg
Sod 110 mg

6 tablespoons
  shortening
1 cup sugar
1 teaspoon vanilla
  extract
1½ teaspoons soda
1 egg
1 cup milk
2 cups flour
5 tablespoons baking
  cocoa

¼ teaspoon salt
½ cup milk
2 tablespoons flour
¼ cup margarine,
  softened
¼ cup shortening
½ cup sugar
1 teaspoon vanilla
  extract

Cream shortening and 1 cup sugar in mixer bowl until light and fluffy. Blend in 1 teaspoon vanilla, soda and egg. Add 1 cup milk, 2 cups flour, cocoa and salt; mix well. Drop by tablespoonfuls 2 inches apart onto ungreased cookie sheet. Bake at 425 degrees for 5 to 6 minutes or until firm. Remove to wire rack to cool. Blend ½ cup milk and 2 table-spoons flour in saucepan. Cook until thickened, stirring constantly. Cream margarine and shortening in mixer bowl for 4 minutes. Add ½ cup sugar; beat for 4 minutes. Add flour mixture and 1 teaspoon vanilla; beat for 4 minutes longer. Spread filling on half the cookies; top with remaining cookies.

BIG SOFT GINGER COOKIES

Yield:
24 servings
Utensil:
cookie sheet

Approx Per
Serving:
Cal 140
Prot 2 g
Carbo 20 g
Fiber <1 g
T Fat 6 g
Chol 9 mg
Sod 108 mg

2¼ cups flour
1 teaspoon soda
1 tablespoon ginger
¾ teaspoon cinnamon
½ teaspoon cloves
¾ cup margarine,
  softened

1 cup sugar
1 egg
¼ cup molasses
2 tablespoons sugar

Sift flour, soda, ginger, cinnamon and cloves together. Cream margarine in large mixer bowl until light. Add 2 cups sugar gradually, beating until fluffy. Blend in egg and molasses. Stir in dry in-gredients. Chill for 2 hours for easier handling. Shape into 1½-inch balls. Roll in 2 tablespoons sugar. Place 2½ inches apart on ungreased cookie sheet. Bake at 350 degrees for 10 minutes or until puffed and light brown; do not overbake. Cool on cookie sheet for 2 minutes. Remove to wire rack to cool completely.

COOKIE PRESS GINGERSNAPS

Yield:
84 servings
Utensil:
cookie sheet

*Approx Per
Serving:*
Cal 46
Prot 1 g
Carbo 7 g
Fiber <1 g
T Fat 2 g
Chol 7 mg
Sod 39 mg

¾ cup butter, softened
¾ cup packed brown
  sugar
¾ cup molasses
1 egg
3 cups sifted flour

1½ teaspoons soda
1 teaspoon cinnamon
1 teaspoon ginger
¼ teaspoon cloves
¼ teaspoon salt
¼ cup sugar sprinkles

Cream butter and brown sugar in mixer bowl until light and fluffy. Blend in molasses and egg. Sift in flour, soda, cinnamon, ginger, cloves and salt; mix well. Spoon into cookie press. Press onto ungreased cookie sheet. Sprinkle with sugar sprinkles. Bake at 375 degrees for 10 to 12 minutes or until golden brown. Remove immediately to wire racks to cool.

HEATH BARS

Yield:
36 servings
Utensil:
2 cookie sheets

*Approx Per
Serving:*
Cal 128
Prot 1 g
Carbo 14 g
Fiber <1 g
T Fat 7 g
Chol 1 mg
Sod 72 mg

36 salted-top saltine
  crackers
½ cup margarine
¾ cup lightly packed
  brown sugar

12 ounces chocolate
  chips
½ cup brickle bits

Arrange crackers salted side up in single layer on 2 cookie sheets. Melt margarine with brown sugar in saucepan. Cook for 3 minutes, stirring constantly. Spread evenly over crackers. Bake at 400 degrees for 5 minutes; remove sooner if edges begin to get too brown. Sprinkle with chocolate chips. Let stand until melted; spread evenly with back of spoon. Sprinkle immediately with brickle bits. Remove crackers to waxed paper to cool. Store in single layer on waxed paper. May place cookie sheet on hot damp towel if crackers become difficult to remove. May reduce brickle bits to ¼ cup.

Italian Biscotti

Yield:
100 servings
Utensil:
cookie sheet

Approx Per
Serving:
Cal 84
Prot 1 g
Carbo 14 g
Fiber <1 g
T Fat 3 g
Chol 13 mg
Sod 28 mg

6 eggs
1/2 cup milk
1 cup oil
4 1-ounce bottles
   anise extract
2 cups sugar

7 cups (about) flour
7 teaspoons baking
   powder
2 cups confectioners'
   sugar
1/4 cup candy sprinkles

Combine eggs, milk, oil and anise extract in mixer bowl; mix until smooth. Add sugar, flour and baking powder; mix to form smooth dough. Shape into small balls; place on cookie sheet sprayed with nonstick cooking spray. Bake at 400 degrees for 10 minutes. Combine confectioners' sugar with enough water to make a thin glaze in bowl; mix well. Dip warm cookies into glaze. Place on wire rack; sprinkle with candy sprinkles.

Nutritional information does not include anise extract.

Italian Brown Balls

Yield:
40 servings
Utensil:
cookie sheet

Approx Per
Serving:
Cal 223
Prot 3 g
Carbo 36 g
Fiber 1 g
T Fat 9 g
Chol 22 mg
Sod 85 mg

4 cups flour
2 cups sugar
1 cup baking cocoa
3 tablespoons baking
   powder
1 tablespoon cinnamon
Salt to taste
1 cup shortening
4 eggs
1 cup milk
2 teaspoons vanilla
   extract

1 cup chopped walnuts
1 1-pound package
   confectioners' sugar
1/4 cup baking cocoa
1 teaspoon cinnamon
1 teaspoon cloves
1 teaspoon vanilla
   extract
1 tablespoon milk
1 teaspoon melted
   shortening

Sift flour, sugar, cocoa, baking powder, cinnamon and salt into bowl. Add 1 cup shortening; work in well. Add eggs, 1 cup milk and 2 teaspoons vanilla; mix well. Add walnuts; knead for 2 minutes. Shape into balls; place on cookie sheet. Bake at 350 degrees for 25 minutes or until wooden pick inserted in center of cookie comes out clean. Cool to room temperature. Combine confectioners' sugar, cocoa, cinnamon and cloves in bowl. Add 1 teaspoon vanilla, 1 tablespoon milk and 1 teaspoon melted shortening; mix well. Spoon over cookies.

SUGAR MOLASSES COOKIES

Yield:
36 servings
Utensil:
cookie sheet

Approx Per Serving:
Cal 110
Prot 1 g
Carbo 17 g
Fiber <1 g
T Fat 5 g
Chol 6 mg
Sod 80 mg

2 cups flour
2 teaspoons soda
1 teaspoon cinnamon
1/2 teaspoon ginger
1/4 teaspoon cloves or
    allspice
1/2 teaspoon salt

3/4 cup shortening
1 cup sugar
1 egg, beaten
1/4 cup molasses
1/4 cup sugar
1 cup confectioners'
    sugar

Sift flour, soda, cinnamon, ginger, cloves and salt together. Cream shortening, 1 cup sugar and egg in mixer bowl until light and smooth. Add molasses and dry ingredients; mix well. Shape by teaspoonfuls into balls; roll in 1/4 cup sugar. Place on cookie sheet. Bake at 375 degrees for 8 to 10 minutes or until golden brown. Roll warm cookies in confectioners' sugar. Cool on wire rack.

OATMEAL COOKIES

Yield:
48 servings
Utensil:
cookie sheet

Approx Per Serving:
Cal 117
Prot 2 g
Carbo 17 g
Fiber 1 g
T Fat 5 g
Chol 9 mg
Sod 77 mg

1 cup shortening
2 cups packed brown
    sugar
2 eggs, beaten
2 teaspoons vanilla
    extract

2 cups sifted flour
1 1/2 teaspoons soda
1 teaspoon salt
3 cups quick-cooking
    oats
1/4 cup sugar

Cream shortening and brown sugar in mixer bowl until light and fluffy. Beat in eggs and vanilla. Sift flour, soda and salt into bowl. Stir in oats. Add to creamed mixture; mix well. Place sugar in small bowl. Shape dough into 1-inch balls with sugar-coated hands. Dip cookie balls into sugar. Place 3 inches apart on greased cookie sheet. Bake at 375 degrees for 12 to 15 minutes or until golden brown. Remove to wire rack to cool.

OATMEAL RAISIN COOKIES

Yield:
54 servings
Utensil:
cookie sheet

*Approx Per
Serving:*
Cal 85
Prot 1 g
Carbo 10 g
Fiber 1 g
T Fat 5 g
Chol 4 mg
Sod 69 mg

1¼ cups margarine,
 softened
½ teaspoon cinnamon
½ teaspoon ginger
½ teaspoon nutmeg
½ teaspoon allspice
1 teaspoon soda
⅓ cup molasses
1 egg

⅓ cup packed brown
 sugar
1 teaspoon vanilla
 extract
Salt to taste
1½ cups flour
3 cups oats
½ to ¾ cup raisins

Combine margarine, cinnamon, ginger, nutmeg, allspice, soda, molasses, egg, brown sugar, vanilla and salt in mixer bowl; mix until smooth. Add flour; mix well. Stir in oats and raisins. Drop onto non-stick cookie sheet. Bake at 375 degrees for 8 to 10 minutes or until golden brown. Remove to wire rack to cool.

GLAZED PEANUT BUTTER SQUARES

Yield:
24 servings
Utensil:
baking pan

*Approx Per
Serving:*
Cal 144
Prot 3 g
Carbo 21 g
Fiber 1 g
T Fat 6 g
Chol 16 mg
Sod 70 mg

⅓ cup butter, softened
⅓ cup peanut butter
3 tablespoons milk
1 egg
2 teaspoons vanilla
 extract
¼ teaspoon salt

2 cups sifted flour
2½ cups (about)
 confectioners' sugar
3 tablespoons peanut
 butter
3 tablespoons (about)
 boiling water

Combine butter, ⅓ cup peanut butter, milk, egg, vanilla and salt in large mixer bowl; beat until smooth. Stir in flour gradually to form stiff batter. Spread evenly in ungreased 9x13-inch baking pan. Bake at 350 degrees for 25 minutes or until top springs back when lightly touched. Combine confectioners' sugar, 3 tablespoons peanut butter and boiling water in large bowl; beat until smooth and of desired consistency. Spoon over warm baked layer. Cool to room temperature. Cut into squares.

CHOCOLATE PEANUT SQUARES

Yield:
48 servings
Utensil:
glass dish

Approx Per Serving:
Cal 136
Prot 2 g
Carbo 11 g
Fiber 1 g
T Fat 10 g
Chol 10 mg
Sod 101 mg

³/₄ cup margarine
2 1-ounce squares semisweet chocolate
1¹/₂ cups graham cracker crumbs
1 cup coconut
¹/₂ cup chopped unsalted peanuts
16 ounces cream cheese, softened
1 cup sugar
1 teaspoon vanilla extract
¹/₄ cup margarine
4 1-ounce squares semisweet chocolate

Combine ³/₄ cup margarine and 2 ounces chocolate in glass bowl. Microwave on High for 1 to 2 minutes or until melted, stirring every 30 seconds. Stir in cracker crumbs, coconut and peanuts. Press into bottom of 9x13-inch glass dish. Chill for 30 minutes. Combine cream cheese, sugar and vanilla in mixer bowl; beat until smooth. Spread over crust. Chill for 30 minutes. Combine ¹/₄ cup margarine and 4 squares chocolate in glass bowl. Microwave on High for 1 to 2 minutes or until melted, stirring every 30 seconds. Spread over cream cheese layer. Chill in refrigerator. Cut into squares.

JEANNE'S PEANUT BUTTER COOKIES

Yield:
24 servings
Utensil:
cookie sheet

Approx Per Serving:
Cal 99
Prot 3 g
Carbo 10 g
Fiber 1 g
T Fat 6 g
Chol 9 mg
Sod 46 mg

1 cup creamy or chunky peanut butter
1 cup sugar
1 egg

Blend peanut butter and sugar in mixer bowl. Beat in egg. Drop by tablespoonfuls onto cookie sheet; flatten with back of spoon. Back at 375 degrees for 8 to 12 minutes or until edges are brown. Remove to wire rack to cool. Store in airtight container.

Peanut Butter Yum-Yums

Yield:
70 servings
Utensil:
glass dish

Approx Per
Serving:
Cal 137
Prot 2 g
Carbo 14 g
Fiber 1 g
T Fat 9 g
Chol 9 mg
Sod 76 mg

1 cup melted butter
1 16-ounce jar peanut butter
2 cups graham crackers crumbs
1 1-pound package confectioners' sugar
12 ounces chocolate chips
1/4 cup butter

Combine 1 cup melted butter, peanut butter, cracker crumbs and confectioners' sugar in bowl; mix until smooth. Spread in 9x13-inch glass dish. Melt chocolate chips with 1/4 cup butter in saucepan. Spread over peanut butter layer. Cut into squares.

Piña Colada Cookies

Yield:
72 servings
Utensil:
cookie sheet

Approx Per
Serving:
Cal 62
Prot 1 g
Carbo 8 g
Fiber <1 g
T Fat 3 g
Chol 6 mg
Sod 57 mg

1 cup margarine, softened
1 cup sugar
1 4-ounce package vanilla instant pudding mix
1 teaspoon vanilla extract
2 eggs
2 1/4 cups flour
1 teaspoon soda
2 individual packets piña colada mix
1 cup shredded coconut

Combine margarine, sugar and pudding mix in large mixer bowl; beat until smooth and creamy. Beat in vanilla and eggs. Add mixture of flour and soda gradually, mixing well. Stir in piña colada mix and coconut; batter will be stiff. Drop by rounded teaspoonfuls 2 inches apart onto ungreased cookie sheet. Bake at 375 degrees for 8 to 10 minutes or until golden brown. Remove to wire rack to cool.

Nutritional information does not include piña colada mix.

PUMPKIN CHEESECAKE BARS

1 cup flour
1/3 cup packed brown
  sugar
5 tablespoons butter,
  softened
1/2 cup chopped
  walnuts
8 ounces cream cheese,
  softened

3/4 cup sugar
1/2 cup pumpkin
2 eggs, slightly beaten
1 1/2 teaspoons
  cinnamon
1 teaspoon allspice
1 teaspoon vanilla
  extract

Mix flour and brown sugar in medium bowl. Cut in butter until crumbly. Stir in walnuts. Reserve 3/4 cup mixture. Press remaining mixture into 8x8-inch baking pan. Bake at 350 degrees for 15 minutes. Combine cream cheese, sugar, pumpkin, eggs, cinnamon, allspice and vanilla in mixer bowl; mix until smooth. Spoon over baked layer. Sprinkle with reserved crumbs. Bake at 350 degrees for 30 to 35 minutes or until golden brown. Cool on wire rack. Cut into 1x2-inch bars.

SCHNECKEN

1/2 cup sugar
1/2 teaspoon cinnamon
2 cups flour
1/2 teaspoon salt
1 cup margarine
1 egg yolk
2/3 cup sour cream

1/4 cup sugar
1/2 teaspoon cinnamon
3/4 cup raisins
3/4 cup chopped
  almonds
1 egg yolk
1 tablespoon milk

Mix 1/2 cup sugar, 1/2 teaspoon cinnamon, flour and salt in bowl. Cut in margarine until mixture resembles cornmeal. Add 1 egg yolk and sour cream; mix well. Shape into 3 balls. Chill in refrigerator overnight. Roll into three 9 to 10-inch circles on floured surface. Cut into 12 wedges. Sprinkle with mixture of 1/4 cup sugar, 1/2 teaspoon cinnamon, raisins and almonds. Roll up wedges from wide end to enclose filling. Place on ungreased cookie sheet. Brush with mixture of 1 egg yolk and milk. Bake at 350 degrees for 20 to 35 minutes or until light brown. Remove to wire rack to cool.

CHOCOLATE FUDGE

Yield:
96 servings
Utensil:
rectangular dish

**Approx Per
Serving:**
Cal 109
Prot 1 g
Carbo 16 g
Fiber <1 g
T Fat 5 g
Chol 1 mg
Sod 17 mg

4¹/₂ cups sugar
1   12-ounce can
     evaporated milk
¹/₂ cup margarine
1   7-ounce jar
     marshmallow creme

24 ounces chocolate
   chips
1 tablespoon vanilla
   extract
2 cups coarsely
   chopped pecans

Line 9x13-inch dish with foil; grease with margarine. Bring sugar, evaporated milk and margarine to a hard boil in saucepan, stirring frequently. Boil for 12 minutes, stirring frequently. Remove from heat. Stir in marshmallow creme, chocolate chips and vanilla until chocolate is melted. Stir in pecans. Pour into prepared dish. Let stand until cool. Cut into squares.

KEVIN'S FOOLPROOF FUDGE

Yield:
77 servings
Utensil:
glass dish

**Approx Per
Serving:**
Cal 65
Prot 1 g
Carbo 7 g
Fiber <1 g
T Fat 4 g
Chol 3 mg
Sod 13 mg

1   14-ounce can
     sweetened
     condensed milk
¹/₄ cup butter

3 cups semisweet
   chocolate chips
1 cup chopped walnuts

Combine condensed milk, butter and chocolate chips in glass dish. Microwave on Medium for 3 to 5 minutes or until melted. Stir in walnuts. Pour into buttered 7x11-inch dish. Chill for 1 hour. Cut into squares.

MÉMÈRE QUINTAL FUDGE

Yield:
77 servings
Utensil:
rectangular dish

2 1-pound packages
   brown sugar
1 tablespoon butter
1 condensed milk can
   whole milk

1 14-ounce can
   sweetened
   condensed milk
1 teaspoon vanilla
   extract

Approx Per
Serving:
Cal 65
Prot 1 g
Carbo 14 g
Fiber 0 g
T Fat 1 g
Chol 3 mg
Sod 15 mg

Combine brown sugar, butter, whole milk and condensed milk in 3-quart saucepan; mix well. Bring to a boil, stirring constantly with wooden spoon. Cook over medium heat for 20 minutes or to 234 to 240 degrees on candy thermometer, soft-ball stage, stirring constantly. Remove from heat. Stir in vanilla. Beat until mixture thickens and loses its luster. Pour into buttered 7x11-inch dish. Let stand until firm. Cut into squares.

MALT BALLS

Yield:
84 servings
Utensil:
bowl

1 cup unsalted butter,
   softened
1 1-pound package
   confectioners' sugar
16 ounces coconut
1/2 cup sweetened
   condensed milk
1 teaspoon vanilla
   extract

1 cup chopped walnuts
4 1-ounce squares
   unsweetened
   chocolate
12 ounces semisweet
   chocolate chips
1 1/2x1x2-inch piece
   paraffin

Approx Per
Serving:
Cal 112
Prot 1 g
Carbo 13 g
Fiber 1 g
T Fat 7 g
Chol 7 mg
Sod 17 mg

Cream butter and confectioners' sugar in mixer bowl until light and fluffy. Stir in coconut, condensed milk, vanilla and walnuts. Chill until slightly firm. Shape into 1-inch balls; insert wooden pick into each ball. Place on cookie sheet. Freeze until firm. Melt chocolate, chocolate chips and paraffin in double boiler over hot water; mix well. Dip balls into chocolate mixture, coating well. Place on waxed paper. Chill until firm. Remove picks; wrap candies individually. May freeze if desired.

PIES AND CAKES

New England Shoreline

APPLE PUFF PIE

Yield:
10 servings
Utensil:
pie plate

Approx Per Serving:
Cal 327
Prot 3 g
Carbo 45 g
Fiber 2 g
T Fat 16 g
Chol 15 mg
Sod 221 mg

4 cups applesauce
1/2 cup sugar
1/4 cup orange juice
2 tablespoons grated orange rind

2 tablespoons quick-cooking tapioca
1 recipe Puff Pie Pastry

Combine applesauce, sugar, orange juice and rind in bowl; mix well. Stir in tapioca. Pour mixture into greased 10-inch pie plate. Arrange puff pastry around edge and in center of pie. Bake at 400 degrees for 25 to 30 minutes or until pastry is brown. Serve warm or cold.

PUFF PIE PASTRY

Yield:
8 servings
Utensil:
pie plate

Approx Per Serving:
Cal 295
Prot 3 g
Carbo 27 g
Fiber 1 g
T Fat 20 g
Chol 18 mg
Sod 273 mg

1 1/2 cups flour
2 teaspoons baking powder
1/2 teaspoon salt
1/2 cup vegetable shortening

2/3 cup milk
1/3 cup sugar
1 1/2 teaspoons nutmeg
1/4 cup melted butter

Sift flour, baking powder and salt into bowl. Cut in shortening until crumbly. Add enough milk to make a soft dough. Shape into small balls. Mix sugar and nutmeg in bowl. Roll balls in melted butter. Roll in sugar mixture to coat.

APPLE PIZZA

1 10-count can
   biscuits
1 cup shredded
   Cheddar cheese
4 apples, peeled, sliced

½ cup packed brown
   sugar
½ teaspoon cinnamon
2 tablespoons flour
2 tablespoons margarine

Separate biscuits; roll into circles. Place on greased baking sheet. Sprinkle with shredded cheese. Place apple slices over cheese. Mix brown sugar, cinnamon and flour together in bowl. Sprinkle over apples. Dot with margarine. Bake at 350 degrees for 15 to 20 minutes. Cool slightly before serving.

CARAMEL CRUNCH APPLE PIE

28 caramels
2 tablespoons water
6 cups sliced, peeled,
   tart cooking apples
1 unbaked 9-inch pie
   shell

¾ cup flour
⅓ cup sugar
½ teaspoon cinnamon
⅓ cup butter
½ cup chopped
   walnuts

Melt caramels in water in top of double boiler over boiling water, stirring occasionally. Layer apples and melted caramels in pie shell. Mix flour, sugar and cinnamon in bowl. Cut in butter until crumbly. Stir in walnuts. Sprinkle over top. Bake at 375 degrees for 40 to 45 minutes.

Impossible French Apple Pie

1/3 cup packed brown sugar
1/2 cup chopped pecans
1 cup baking mix
3 tablespoons butter
6 cups sliced, peeled tart apples
1/2 teaspoon cinnamon
1/4 teaspoon nutmeg
3/4 cup milk
2 tablespoons butter, softened
2 eggs
1/2 cup baking mix
1 cup sugar

Combine brown sugar, pecans and baking mix in bowl. Cut in 3 tablespoons butter until crumbly. Combine apple slices, cinnamon and nutmeg in bowl; toss to coat apples with spices. Place in greased pie plate. Sprinkle with brown sugar mixture. Combine milk, 2 tablespoons butter, eggs, baking mix and sugar in blender container. Process for 1 minute. Pour over apples. Bake at 325 degrees for 55 to 65 minutes or until knife inserted near center comes out clean.

New-Fashioned Apple Pie

1/2 cup raisins
3 tablespoons orange flavored liqueur
1 recipe 2-crust pie pastry
1/4 cup plus 2 tablespoons sugar
1/4 cup plus 2 tablespoons packed brown sugar
1 tablespoon cornstarch
1 tablespoon lemon juice
1 teaspoon cinnamon
6 cups peeled, sliced cooking apples
3 tablespoons butter
1 egg yolk
2 tablespoons water

Combine raisins and liqueur in small bowl; mix well. Line 9-inch pie plate with 1 pie pastry. Combine sugar, brown sugar, cornstarch, lemon juice and cinnamon in bowl; mix well. Add apples; toss to coat. Stir in raisin mixture. Spoon into pastry-lined pie plate. Dot with butter. Cover with remaining pie pastry, sealing edges; cut air vents. Beat egg yolk and water in bowl. Brush over top. Bake at 450 degrees for 40 to 50 minutes or until golden brown.

PAPER BAG APPLE PIE

Yield:
8 servings
Utensil:
pie plate

Approx Per
Serving:
Cal 358
Prot 3 g
Carbo 61 g
Fiber 2 g
T Fat 12 g
Chol 12 mg
Sod 214 mg

¾ cup sugar
2 tablespoons flour
1 teaspoon lemon juice
½ teaspoon cinnamon
½ teaspoon nutmeg
6 cups sliced, peeled
   tart cooking apples
1 unbaked 9-inch pie
   shell
½ cup flour
½ cup packed brown
   sugar
⅛ teaspoon salt
3 tablespoons butter

Mix sugar, 2 tablespoons flour, lemon juice, cinnamon and nutmeg in bowl. Add apple slices; toss to coat. Spoon into pie shell. Combine ½ cup flour, brown sugar and salt in bowl; mix well. Cut in butter until crumbly. Sprinkle over apples. Place pie in large brown paper bag made of non-recycled material; fold open end over 2 times and seal. Bake at 400 degrees for 40 to 50 minutes or until brown.

DOUBLE CHOCOLATE PIE

Yield:
8 servings
Utensil:
pie plate

Approx Per
Serving:
Cal 413
Prot 5 g
Carbo 34 g
Fiber 1 g
T Fat 30 g
Chol 141 mg
Sod 216 mg

1¼ cups chocolate
   wafer crumbs
¼ cup sugar
⅓ cup melted butter
1 cup chocolate chips
1 egg
2 egg yolks
1½ teaspoons dark
   rum
2 egg whites, stiffly
   beaten
1 cup whipped cream

Combine cookie crumbs, sugar and butter in bowl; mix well. Press into bottom and up sides of greased 10-inch pie plate. Bake at 400 degrees for 5 minutes. Chill in refrigerator. Melt chocolate chips in top of double boiler; remove from heat. Add egg, egg yolks and rum; beat well. Fold in egg whites and whipped cream. Spoon into pie shell. Chill until serving time. Garnish with additional whipped cream and shaved chocolate.

CHOCOLATE RASPBERRY TARTS

Yield:
4 servings
Utensil:
tray

Approx Per Serving:
Cal 658
Prot 7 g
Carbo 55 g
Fiber 2 g
T Fat 48 g
Chol 62 mg
Sod 341 mg

8 ounces cream cheese, softened
8 ounces semisweet chocolate chips, melted

2 tablespoons raspberry liqueur
1 4-ounce package graham cracker tart shells

Combine cream cheese, melted chocolate and raspberry liqueur in bowl; mix well. Spoon into graham cracker tart shells. Garnish each serving with raspberries and mint sprigs. Place on tray. Chill until serving time.

CHOCOLATE TORTE ROYALE

Yield:
8 servings
Utensil:
baking sheet

Approx Per Serving:
Cal 302
Prot 3 g
Carbo 32 g
Fiber 1 g
T Fat 20 g
Chol 94 mg
Sod 96 mg

2 egg whites
1/2 teaspoon vinegar
1/2 cup sugar
1/4 teaspoon cinnamon
1/4 teaspoon salt
1 cup semisweet chocolate chips

2 egg yolks, beaten
1/4 cup water
1 cup whipping cream
1/4 cup sugar
1/4 teaspoon cinnamon

Cover baking sheet with baking parchment. Draw 8-inch circle in center of parchment. Beat egg whites with vinegar until soft peaks form. Add 1/2 cup sugar, 1/4 teaspoon cinnamon and salt, beating until stiff peaks form. Spread meringue 1/2 inch thick inside circle and 1 3/4 inches high around edge. Bake at 275 degrees for 1 hour. Turn off oven. Let stand in oven for 2 hours. Remove; peel off paper. Melt chocolate chips in double boiler over hot water. Cool slightly. Spread 2 tablespoons melted chocolate over bottom of meringue shell. Add egg yolks and water to remaining chocolate; mix well. Chill mixture until thick. Beat whipping cream until soft peaks form. Add 1/4 cup sugar and 1/4 teaspoon cinnamon gradually, beating until stiff. Layer half the whipped cream, all the chocolate mixture and remaining whipped cream in meringue shell. Chill for several hours before serving. Garnish with additional whipped cream and pecans.

GRASSHOPPER PIE

Yield:
8 servings
Utensil:
pie plate

Approx Per
Serving:
Cal 353
Prot 2 g
Carbo 41 g
Fiber 1 g
T Fat 19 g
Chol 41 mg
Sod 222 mg

24 chocolate wafers, finely crushed
1/4 cup melted margarine
2 cups whipped cream

1 7-ounce jar marshmallow creme
1/4 cup Crème de Menthe

Combine wafer crumbs and margarine in bowl; mix well. Reserve 2 cups mixture. Press remaining mixture into bottom and up sides of greased 9-inch pie plate. Fold whipped cream and marshmallow creme together in bowl. Fold in Crème de Menthe. Spoon into prepared pie plate. Sprinkle with reserved crumb mixture. Freeze until firm.

LEMON PINEAPPLE PIE

Yield:
8 servings
Utensil:
pie plate

Approx Per
Serving:
Cal 415
Prot 3 g
Carbo 73 g
Fiber 2 g
T Fat 14 g
Chol 2 mg
Sod 466 mg

1 20-ounce can crushed pineapple
1 3-ounce package lemon instant pudding mix

1 2-ounce package whipped topping mix
1 9-inch graham cracker pie shell

Combine undrained pineapple and pudding mix in bowl; mix well. Prepare whipped topping mix using package directions. Fold into pudding mixture. Spoon into graham cracker pie shell. Chill for several hours to overnight. Garnish with lemon slices twisted into S shape.

OREO CREAM PIE

Yield:
8 servings
Utensil:
pie plate

Approx Per
Serving:
Cal 531
Prot 4 g
Carbo 56 g
Fiber 1 g
T Fat 33 g
Chol 79 mg
Sod 332 mg

41 Oreo cookies
1/4 cup melted butter
24 marshmallows

1/2 cup milk
1 1/2 cups whipping
cream, whipped

Chop 10 cookies coarsely. Crush 25 cookies finely. Combine finely crushed cookies with butter in bowl; mix well. Press into bottom and up sides of 9-inch pie plate. Chill in refrigerator. Combine marshmallows and milk in 2-quart saucepan. Heat until marshmallows are dissolved, stirring constantly. Cool to room temperature. Fold in 2 cups whipped cream. Fold in chopped cookies. Spoon into prepared pie plate. Chill for 4 hours or until firm. Garnish with remaining whipped cream and cookies.

RED VELVET PIE

Yield:
8 servings
Utensil:
pie plate

Approx Per
Serving:
Cal 373
Prot 4 g
Carbo 41 g
Fiber 2 g
T Fat 22 g
Chol 52 mg
Sod 214 mg

1 3-ounce package
raspberry gelatin
1 1/4 cups boiling water
1/4 cup sugar
1 tablespoon lemon
juice
1 10-ounce package
frozen raspberries
1 baked 10-inch pie
shell

3 ounces cream cheese,
softened
1/3 cup confectioners'
sugar
1 teaspoon vanilla
extract
1 cup whipping cream,
whipped

Dissolve gelatin in boiling water in bowl. Add sugar, lemon juice and raspberries; mix well. Pour into baked pie shell. Chill for several hours or until set. Combine cream cheese, confectioners' sugar and vanilla in bowl; beat well. Fold in whipped cream. Spread over congealed layer. Chill until serving time.

Strawberry Pie

Yield:
8 servings
Utensil:
pie plate

Approx Per
Serving:
Cal 231
Prot 2 g
Carbo 40 g
Fiber 1 g
T Fat 8 g
Chol 0 mg
Sod 152 mg

¾ cup sugar
2 tablespoons light
    corn syrup
2 tablespoons
    cornstarch
1 cup water
3 tablespoons
    strawberry gelatin

Red food coloring to
    taste
2 cups (or more)
    strawberries
1 baked 9-inch pie
    shell

Combine sugar, corn syrup, cornstarch and water in saucepan; mix well. Bring to a boil. Simmer until mixture is clear and thickened, stirring constantly. Remove from heat. Stir in gelatin until dissolved. Add food coloring until desired color. Chill until partially congealed. Fold in strawberries. Spoon into pie shell. Chill until serving time.

Apple Cake

Yield:
12 servings
Utensil:
tube pan

Approx Per
Serving:
Cal 627
Prot 6 g
Carbo 74 g
Fiber 3 g
T Fat 36 g
Chol 53 mg
Sod 266 mg

1½ cups oil
2 cups sugar
3 eggs
3 cups flour
1 teaspoon salt
1 teaspoon cinnamon

1 teaspoon soda
1 teaspoon vanilla
    extract
1 cup raisins
1 cup chopped pecans
3 cups chopped apples

Cream oil and sugar in mixer bowl until light and fluffy. Add eggs 1 at a time, beating well after each addition. Mix flour, salt, cinnamon and soda together. Add to batter; mix well. Stir in vanilla, raisins, pecans and apples. Spoon into greased and floured tube pan. Bake at 350 degrees for 1 hour and 15 minutes or until cake tests done. Cool in pan for several minutes. Invert onto wire rack to cool completely.

APPLESAUCE SPICE CAKE

1 cup unsalted butter, softened
2 cups sugar
2 cups applesauce
3 cups flour
1 3/4 teaspoons soda
1 teaspoon cinnamon
1 teaspoon nutmeg
1/2 teaspoon mace
1 cup chopped walnuts
1 cup raisins
1 teaspoon vanilla extract
Brown Sugar Frosting

Grease 9-inch tube pan. Line with waxed paper; grease waxed paper. Cream butter and sugar in mixer bowl until light and fluffy. Add applesauce; mix well. Sift flour, soda, cinnamon, nutmeg and mace together. Reserve 1/4 cup flour mixture. Add remaining flour mixture to batter; mix well. Mix walnuts, raisins and reserved flour mixture together. Add to batter. Add vanilla; mix well. Spoon into prepared tube pan. Bake at 325 degrees for 1 1/2 to 1 3/4 hours or until cake tests done. Cool in pan for several minutes. Loosen cake from sides of pan. Invert onto wire rack to cool completely. Pour hot Brown Sugar Frosting over cooled cake, allowing icing to run down sides of cake. The frosting will harden very quickly.

BROWN SUGAR FROSTING

1 1/2 cups packed light brown sugar
6 tablespoons whipping cream
1/4 cup unsalted butter
1 teaspoon vanilla extract
3/4 cup confectioners' sugar

Combine brown sugar, whipping cream and butter in saucepan. Bring to a full rolling boil over medium heat, stirring occasionally until smooth. Remove from heat. Stir in vanilla and confectioners' sugar. Use immediately as frosting will harden very quickly.

Danish Apple Cake

Yield:
14 servings
Utensil:
cake pan

Approx Per
Serving:
Cal 227
Prot 3 g
Carbo 26 g
Fiber 1 g
T Fat 13 g
Chol 77 mg
Sod 124 mg

¾ cup butter, softened
¾ cup sugar
3 eggs
1 teaspoon vanilla
  extract
½ teaspoon baking
  powder
1½ cups flour
2 apples, peeled, sliced
2 tablespoons melted
  butter
2 tablespoons sugar
Cinnamon to taste

Cream ¾ cup butter and ¾ cup sugar in mixer bowl until light and fluffy. Add eggs 1 at a time, beating well after each addition. Add vanilla; mix well. Mix baking powder and flour together. Add to batter; mix well. Spoon into buttered 9x11-inch cake pan. Arrange apples over top in rows; drizzle with 2 tablespoons butter. Sprinkle with 2 tablespoons sugar and cinnamon. Bake at 400 degrees for 30 to 35 minutes or until cake tests done.

Old-Fashioned Nut Cake

Yield:
12 servings
Utensil:
tube pan

Approx Per
Serving:
Cal 429
Prot 7 g
Carbo 52 g
Fiber 1 g
T Fat 22 g
Chol 73 mg
Sod 287 mg

¾ cup shortening
1½ cups sugar
4 egg yolks
3 cups flour
3 teaspoons baking
  powder
1 teaspoon salt
1 cup chopped walnuts
¾ cup milk
4 egg whites
2 teaspoons vanilla
  extract

Cream shortening and sugar in mixer bowl until light and fluffy. Add egg yolks; mix well. Sift flour, baking powder and salt together. Mix a small amount of flour mixture with walnuts in bowl. Add remaining flour mixture to batter; mix well. Add milk; mix well. Beat egg whites until soft peaks form. Add vanilla; beat until stiff. Fold into batter. Fold in walnuts. Spoon into greased and floured 10-inch tube pan. Bake at 350 degrees for 35 to 45 minutes or until cake tests done. Cool in pan for several minutes. Invert onto wire rack to cool completely. Frost with favorite frosting.

HAVERHILL BANANA FUDGE RING

Yield:
12 servings
Utensil:
tube pan

Approx Per
Serving:
Cal 665
Prot 6 g
Carbo 81 g
Fiber 1 g
T Fat 36 g
Chol 125 mg
Sod 463 mg

1 2-layer package
   chocolate fudge
   cake mix
1 4-ounce package
   chocolate instant
   pudding mix

4 eggs
1 cup water
1/2 cup mashed banana
1/4 cup vegetable oil
Banana Cream Frosting

Combine cake mix, pudding mix and eggs in mixer bowl; mix well. Add water, banana and oil. Beat at medium speed for 8 minutes. Spoon batter into greased and lightly floured 10-inch tube pan. Bake at 350 degrees for 45 to 50 minutes or until cake tests done. Cool in pan for 15 minutes. Invert onto serving plate. Spread Banana Cream Frosting over side and top of cake. Chill until serving time.

BANANA CREAM FROSTING

Yield:
12 servings
Utensil:
bowl

Approx Per
Serving:
Cal 372
Prot 2 g
Carbo 34 g
Fiber 1 g
T Fat 26 g
Chol 54 mg
Sod 114 mg

1 package buttercream
   milk chocolate
   frosting mix

2 cups whipping cream
1/2 cup mashed banana
1/2 cup chopped pecans

Combine frosting mix and whipping cream in mixer bowl; beat until thickened. Add banana; mix well. Stir in pecans.

LEMON POPPY SEED CAKE

1 cup butter, softened
1½ cups sugar
2 tablespoons grated
 lemon rind
3 tablespoons lemon
 juice
½ teaspoon vanilla
 extract
4 eggs
2 tablespoons poppy
 seed
3 cups flour
½ teaspoon salt
½ teaspoon baking
 powder
½ teaspoon soda
1 cup lemon yogurt
Lemon Frosting

Cream butter and sugar in mixer bowl until light and fluffy. Add lemon rind, lemon juice, vanilla, eggs and poppy seed; mix well. Sift flour, salt, baking powder and soda together. Add to batter; mix well. Add yogurt; beat well. Spoon into greased and floured tube pan. Bake at 350 degrees for 55 to 60 minutes or until cake tests done. Cool in pan for several minutes. Invert onto serving plate. Spread Lemon Frosting over top and side of cake.

LEMON FROSTING

½ cup butter, softened
1 1-pound package
 confectioners' sugar
1 tablespoon lemon
 juice
1 tablespoon milk
½ teaspoon vanilla
 extract
1 tablespoon grated
 lemon rind

Cream butter and confectioners' sugar in mixer bowl. Add lemon juice, milk, vanilla and lemon rind; beat until smooth.

WACKY CHOCOLATE CAKE

Yield:
15 servings
Utensil:
cake pan

Approx Per Serving:
Cal 298
Prot 3 g
Carbo 47 g
Fiber 1 g
T Fat 12 g
Chol 0 mg
Sod 182 mg

¾ cup oil
2 cups sugar
3 cups flour
6 tablespoons (heaping) baking cocoa
2 teaspoons soda
½ teaspoon salt
2 tablespoons vinegar
2 teaspoons vanilla extract
2 cups water

Cream oil and sugar in mixer bowl until light and fluffy. Mix flour, cocoa, soda and salt together. Add to mixture. Add vanilla and water; mix well. Spoon into greased and floured 9x13-inch cake pan. Bake at 350 degrees for 30 minutes or until cake tests done.

WHITE TURTLE CAKE

Yield:
12 servings
Utensil:
cake pan

Approx Per Serving:
Cal 690
Prot 8 g
Carbo 85 g
Fiber 1 g
T Fat 37 g
Chol 66 mg
Sod 404 mg

1 2-layer package yellow cake mix
1 cup water
½ 14-ounce can sweetened condensed milk
1 cup vegetable oil
3 eggs
½ 14-ounce can sweetened condensed milk
1 14-ounce package caramels
1 cup chopped pecans
½ cup melted margarine
1 1-pound package confectioners' sugar
6 tablespoons milk
1 teaspoon vanilla extract

Combine cake mix, water, ½ can sweetened condensed milk, oil and eggs in mixer bowl; beat well. Spread half the batter in greased 9x13-inch cake pan. Bake at 350 degrees for 30 minutes. Combine remaining ½ can sweetened condensed milk and caramels in saucepan. Heat until caramels are melted, stirring frequently. Stir in pecans. Pour over hot cake. Spread remaining batter over caramel layer. Bake for 20 minutes longer. Combine margarine, confectioners' sugar and milk in mixer bowl; beat well. Add vanilla; mix well. Spread frosting on warm cake.

KID'S KORNER

Balloon Festival
Quechee, Vermont

EGG IN-A-FRAME

1 slice bread
1 teaspoon butter
1 egg
1 teaspoon butter

* **Cut** circle in center of bread with rim of drinking glass.

* **Melt** 1 teaspoon butter in small skillet over low heat.

* **Place** bread in skillet.

* **Break** egg into small container; slide into center of bread.

* **Cook** until bread is golden brown on bottom. Lift carefully.

* **Place** remaining 1 teaspoon butter in skillet.

* **Turn** egg and bread uncooked side down in skillet.

* **Cook** for 1 to 2 minutes longer until egg is done to taste.

* **Yield:** 1 serving.

HOT DIGGETY DOGS

1   8-count can crescent rolls
8 hot dogs
4 slices American cheese,
    cut into triangles

* **Preheat** oven to 400 degrees.

* **Unroll** crescent rolls; separate into triangles.

* **Place** 1 hot dog and 1 triangle of cheese on wide end of roll.

* **Roll** to enclose hot dog and cheese; place point-side down on lightly greased baking sheet.

* **Bake** for 10 minutes or until golden brown.

* **Serve** hot with mustard, mayonnaise and pickles.

* **Yield:** 8 servings.

MINIATURE PIZZAS

3/4 cup catsup
48 Melba toast rounds
2 ounces thinly sliced
    pepperoni
1 cup shredded mozzarella
    cheese
Oregano to taste

* **Spread** catsup on toast rounds.

* **Top** with pepperoni; sprinkle with cheese.

* **Sprinkle** with oregano.

* **Place** on ungreased baking sheet.

* **Bake** at 400 for 3 minutes or until cheese is melted.

* **Yield:** 48 small pizzas.

Peanut Butter-Stuffed Apples

4 apples
$\frac{1}{2}$ cup peanut butter
2 tablespoons raisins
2 tablespoons granola
1 tablespoon oats
2 tablespoons honey

* **Cut** cores from apples.

* **Combine** peanut butter, raisins, granola, oats and honey in small bowl; mix well.

* **Spoon** 2 tablespoons peanut butter mixture into each apple.

* **Wrap** in foil. Eat whole or sliced.

* **Chill** until serving time.

* **Yield:** 4 servings.

Zoo Cage Salads

1 orange, cut into ½-inch slices
Toothpicks, Parsley
1 banana
3 ounces cream cheese, softened
Crushed cereal, raisins,
    shredded carrot, almonds,
    licorice

* **Attach** orange slices with toothpicks to form cages. Sprinkle parsley inside cages.

* **Cut** slice of banana ½-inch long for owl. Spread cream cheese on all sides; roll in cereal to coat. Attach 2 raisins with cream cheese for ears. Attach small pieces of carrot with cream cheese for eyes. Use almond for nose. Place in cage.

* **Cut** small slice of banana for mouse. Brush banana with lemon juice. Attach sliced almonds with cream cheese for ears; use bits of raisins for eyes. Attach licorice with cream cheese for tail and whiskers.

* **Yield:** 1 serving.

Hawaiian Toast

8 slices white bread
8 slices pineapple
8 $\frac{1}{8}$-inch slices ham
8 slices Cheddar cheese

* **Preheat** broiler.

* **Place** bread slices on baking sheet.

* **Layer** 1 slice pineapple, 1 slice ham and 1 slice cheese on each bread slice.

* **Cook** under hot broiler until cheese is melted.

* **Yield:** 4 servings.

A-B-C Pancakes

1¼ cups sifted flour
1½ teaspoons baking powder
¾ teaspoon salt
1 tablespoon sugar
1 egg, beaten
½ cup milk
3 tablespoons oil

* **Sift** flour, baking powder, salt and sugar together.

* **Combine** egg, milk and oil in mixer bowl; mix well.

* **Add** flour mixture, stirring until just mixed.

* **Drizzle** 1 teaspoonful batter onto hot greased griddle to form letters of the alphabet.

* **Cook** until golden brown on both sides, turning carefully.

* **Ladle** remaining batter over and around cooked letters, making pancakes of desired size.

* **Cook** until golden brown on both sides, turning once.

* **Serve** with butter and pancake syrup.

* **Yield:** 12 pancakes.

ANGELS ON HORSEBACK

8 whole graham crackers
4 1½-ounce chocolate
   candy bars
12 marshmallows

* **Preheat** broiler.

* **Place** 4 whole graham crackers on baking sheet.

* **Top** each with chocolate candy bar.

* **Cook** under hot broiler until chocolate starts to melt.

* **Place** 3 marshmallows on each chocolate bar.

* **Broil** until marshmallows are slightly brown and puffy.

* **Remove** from oven.

* **Top** with remaining graham crackers.

* **Serve** warm with a glass of milk.

* **Yield:** 4 servings.

PEANUT BUTTER CANDY

½ cup cold water
1 box confectioners' sugar
1½ cups peanut butter
1 7-ounce jar marshmallow
  creme
⅛ teaspoon vanilla extract

* **Combine** cold water and confectioners' sugar in saucepan; mix well.

* **Boil** for 5 minutes, stirring constantly.

* **Remove** from heat.

* **Add** peanut butter, marshmallow creme and vanilla; mix quickly.

* **Spread** in buttered 9x13-inch dish.

* **Chill** until firm. Cut into squares.

* **Yield:** 20 servings.

COCONUT SNOWBALLS

Several drops of food coloring
¹/₂ teaspoon milk
1¹/₃ cups coconut
1 quart ice cream

* **Combine** food coloring of desired color and milk in large bowl; mix well.

* **Add** coconut, tossing with fork to tint coconut evenly.

* **Scoop** ice cream into balls; roll in coconut to coat.

* **Place** in desert dishes. Serve immediately.

* **May** place coconut balls in 9x13-inch pan.

* **Freeze**, tightly covered, until serving time.

* **Yield:** 8 servings.

Cupcake Cones

1   2-layer package cake mix
24 flat-bottom ice cream cones
1   16-ounce can frosting
Candy sprinkles

* **Prepare** cake mix using package directions.

* **Fill** ice cream cones ⅓ full.

* **Place** on baking sheet.

* **Bake** using package directions for 20 to 25 minutes or until cakes tests done.

* **Remove** to wire rack to cool.

* **Spread** frosting over cooled cupcakes, swirling frosting into point at center of top.

* **Sprinkle** with candy sprinkles.

* **Yield:** 24 cupcake cones.

ICE CREAM BANANA PUDDING

> 1 4-ounce package vanilla
>   instant pudding mix
> 2 cups milk
> 1 12-ounce package vanilla
>   wafers
> 3 or 4 bananas, sliced
> 1 pint vanilla ice cream
> 8 ounces whipped topping

* **Prepare** vanilla pudding with milk using package directions.

* **Chill** until thickened.

* **Place** several vanilla wafers in bottom and around sides of 6 dessert dishes.

* **Spoon** pudding into dishes.

* **Add** layer of bananas and 1 scoop of ice cream.

* **Top** with whipped topping.

* **Serve** immediately.

* **Yield:** 6 servings.

EDIBLE PLAY DOUGH

1 cup peanut butter
1 cup corn syrup
1¼ cups confectioners' sugar
1¼ cups nonfat dry milk
　　powder

* **Combine** peanut butter and corn syrup in large bowl; mix well.

* **Combine** confectioners' sugar and dry milk in bowl; mix well.

* **Add** to peanut butter mixture; mix well.

* **Add** additional confectioners' sugar if needed to make consistency of play dough.

* Shape as desired. May be eaten.

* **Yields:** 2½ to 3 cups.

CHILDREN'S PLAY DOUGH

1 cup salt
4 to 5 cups flour
1 cup (about) water
Several drops of food coloring

* **Combine** salt and flour in bowl; mix well.

* **Add** water a small amount at a time, mixing until smooth and elastic.

* **Add** food coloring, mixing until of desired color.

* Do not eat this play dough!

* **Yield:** 5 to 6 cups.

EQUIVALENT CHART

	When the recipe calls for	Use
Baking	½ cup butter 2 cups butter 4 cups all-purpose flour 4½ to 5 cups sifted cake flour 1 square chocolate 1 cup semisweet chocolate chips 4 cups marshmallows 2¼ cups packed brown sugar 4 cups confectioners' sugar 2 cups granulated sugar	4 ounces 1 pound 1 pound 1 pound 1 ounce 6 ounces 1 pound 1 pound 1 pound 1 pound
Cereal – Bread	1 cup fine dry bread crumbs 1 cup soft bread crumbs 1 cup small bread cubes 1 cup fine cracker crumbs 1 cup fine graham cracker crumbs 1 cup vanilla wafer crumbs 1 cup crushed cornflakes 4 cups cooked macaroni 3½ cups cooked rice	4 to 5 slices 2 slices 2 slices 28 saltines 15 crackers 22 wafers 3 cups uncrushed 8 ounces uncooked 1 cup uncooked
Dairy	1 cup shredded cheese 1 cup cottage cheese 1 cup sour cream 1 cup whipped cream ⅔ cup evaporated milk 1⅔ cups evaporated milk	4 ounces 8 ounces 8 ounces ½ cup heavy cream 1 small can 1 13-ounce can

Fruit	4 cups sliced or chopped apples
	1 cup mashed bananas
	2 cups pitted cherries
	2½ cups shredded coconut
	4 cups cranberries
	1 cup pitted dates
	1 cup candied fruit
	3 to 4 tablespoons lemon juice plus
	   1 tablespoon grated lemon rind
	⅓ cup orange juice plus 2 teaspoons
	   grated orange rind
	4 cups sliced peaches
	2 cups pitted prunes
	3 cups raisins
		4 medium
		3 medium
		4 cups unpitted
		8 ounces
		1 pound
		1 8-ounce package
		1 8-ounce package
		1 lemon
		
		1 orange
		
		8 medium
		1 12-ounce package
		1 15-ounce package

When the recipe calls for	Use
Meats 4 cups chopped cooked chicken 3 cups chopped cooked meat 2 cups cooked ground meat	1 5-pound chicken 1 pound, cooked 1 pound, cooked
Nuts 1 cup chopped nuts	4 ounces shelled 1 pound unshelled
Vegetables 2 cups cooked green beans 2½ cups lima beans or red beans 4 cups shredded cabbage 1 cup grated carrot 8 ounces fresh mushrooms 1 cup chopped onion 4 cups sliced or chopped potatoes 2 cups canned tomatoes	½ pound fresh or 1 16-ounce can 1 cup dried, cooked 1 pound 1 large 1 4-ounce can 1 large 4 medium 1 16-ounce can

Measurement Equivalents

1 tablespoon = 3 teaspoons
2 tablespoons = 1 ounce
4 tablespoons = ¼ cup
5⅓ tablespoons = ⅓ cup
8 tablespoons = ½ cup
12 tablespoons = ¾ cup
16 tablespoons = 1 cup
1 cup = 8 ounces or ½ pint
4 cups = 1 quart
4 quarts = 1 gallon

1 6½ to 8-ounce can = 1 cup
1 10½ to 12-ounce can = 1¼ cups
1 14 to 16-ounce can = 1¾ cups
1 16 to 17-ounce can = 2 cups
1 18 to 20-ounce can = 2½ cups
1 29-ounce can = 3½ cups
1 46 to 51-ounce can = 5¾ cups
1 6½ to 7½-pound can or
   Number 10 = 12 to 13 cups

Metric Equivalents

Liquid	Dry
1 teaspoon = 5 milliliters 1 tablespoon = 15 milliliters 1 fluid ounce = 30 milliliters 1 cup = 250 milliliters 1 pint = 500 milliliters	1 quart = 1 liter 1 ounce = 30 grams 1 pound = 450 grams 2.2 pounds = 1 kilogram

*NOTE: The metric measures are approximate benchmarks for
purposes of home food preparation.*

SUBSTITUTION CHART

	Instead of	Use
Baking	1 teaspoon baking powder 1 tablespoon cornstarch (for thickening) 1 cup sifted all-purpose flour 1 cup sifted cake flour	¼ teaspoon soda plus ½ teaspoon cream of tartar 2 tablespoons flour or 1 tablespoon tapioca 1 cup plus 2 tablespoons sifted cake flour 1 cup minus 2 tablespoons sifted all-purpose flour
	1 cup dry bread crumbs	¾ cup cracker crumbs
Dairy	1 cup buttermilk 1 cup heavy cream 1 cup light cream 1 cup sour cream 1 cup sour milk	1 cup sour milk or 1 cup yogurt ¾ cup skim milk plus ⅓ cup butter ⅞ cup skim milk plus 3 tablespoons butter ⅞ cup sour milk plus 3 tablespoons butter 1 cup milk plus 1 tablespoon vinegar or lemon juice or 1 cup buttermilk
Seasoning	1 teaspoon allspice 1 cup catsup 1 clove of garlic 1 teaspoon Italian spice 1 teaspoon lemon juice 1 tablespoon mustard 1 medium onion	½ teaspoon cinnamon plus ⅛ teaspoon cloves 1 cup tomato sauce plus ½ cup sugar plus 2 tablespoons vinegar ⅛ teaspoon garlic powder or ⅛ teaspoon instant minced garlic or ¾ teaspoon garlic salt or 5 drops of liquid garlic ¼ teaspoon each oregano, basil, thyme, rosemary plus dash of cayenne ½ teaspoon vinegar 1 teaspoon dry mustard 1 tablespoon dried minced onion or 1 teaspoon onion powder
Sweet	1 1-ounce square chocolate 1⅔ ounces semisweet chocolate 1 cup honey 1 cup granulated sugar	¼ cup cocoa plus 1 teaspoon shortening 1 ounce unsweetened chocolate plus 4 teaspoons granulated sugar 1 to 1¼ cups sugar plus ¼ cup liquid or 1 cup corn syrup or molasses 1 cup packed brown sugar or 1 cup corn syrup, molasses or honey minus ¼ cup liquid

NUTRITIONAL GUIDELINES

The editors have attempted to present these family recipes in a form that allows approximate nutritional values to be computed. Persons with dietary or health problems or whose diets require close monitoring should not rely solely on the nutritional information provided. They should consult their physicians or a registered dietitian for specific information.

Abbreviations for Nutritional Analysis

Cal — Calories	Dietary Fiber — Fiber	Sod — Sodium
Prot — Protein	T Fat — Total Fat	gr — gram
Carbo — Carbohydrates	Chol — Cholesterol	mg — milligrams

Nutritional information for these recipes is computed from information derived from many sources, including materials supplied by the United States Department of Agriculture, computer databanks and journals in which the information is assumed to be in the public domain. However, many specialty items, new products and processed foods may not be available from these sources or may vary from the average values used in these analyses. More information on new and/or specific products may be obtained by reading the nutrient labels. Unless otherwise specified, the nutritional analysis of these recipes is based on all measurements being level.

- **Artificial sweeteners** vary in use and strength so should be used "to taste," using the recipe ingredients as a guideline.
- **Artificial sweeteners** using aspartame (NutraSweet and Equal) should not be used as a sweetener in recipes involving prolonged heating which reduces the sweet taste. For further information on the use of these sweeteners, refer to package information.
- **Alcoholic ingredients** have been analyzed for the basic ingredients, although cooking causes the evaporation of alcohol thus decreasing caloric content.
- **Buttermilk, sour cream** and **yogurt** are the types available commercially.
- **Cake mixes** which are prepared using package directions include 3 eggs and ½ cup oil.
- **Chicken,** cooked for boning and chopping, has been roasted; this method yields the lowest caloric values.
- **Cottage cheese** is cream-style with 4.2% creaming mixture. Dry-curd cottage cheese has no creaming mixture.
- **Eggs** are all large.
- **Flour** is unsifted all-purpose flour.
- **Garnishes,** serving suggestions and other optional additions and variations are not included in the analysis.
- **Margarine** and **butter** are regular, not whipped or presoftened.
- **Milk** is whole milk, 3.5% butterfat. Lowfat milk is 1% butterfat. Evaporated milk is whole milk with 60% of the water removed.
- **Oil** is any type of vegetable cooking oil. Shortening is hydrogenated vegetable shortening.
- **Salt** and other ingredients to taste as noted in the ingredients have not been included in the nutritional analysis.
- If a choice of ingredients has been given, the nutritional analysis reflects the first option.

Herbs and Spices

Allspice
Pungent aromatic spice, whole or in powdered form. It is excellent in marinades, particularly in game marinade, or in curries.

Basil
Can be chopped and added to cold poultry salads. If the recipe calls for tomatoes or tomato sauce, add a touch of basil to bring out a rich flavor.

Bay leaf
The basis of many French seasonings. It is added to soups, stews, marinades and stuffings.

Bouquet garni
A must in many Creole cuisine recipes. It is a bundle of herbs, spices and bay leaf tied together and added to soups, stews or sauces.

Celery seed
From wild celery rather than domestic celery. It adds pleasant flavor to bouillon or a stock base.

Chervil
One of the traditional *fines herbes* used in French-derived cooking. (The others are tarragon, parsley and chives.) It is good in omelets or soups.

Chives
Available fresh, dried or frozen, it can be substituted for raw onion or shallot in any poultry recipe.

Cinnamon
Ground from the bark of the cinnamon tree, it is important in desserts as well as savory dishes.

Coriander
Adds an unusual flavor to soups, stews, chili dishes, curries and some desserts.

Cumin
A staple spice in Mexican cooking. To use, rub seeds together and let them fall into the dish just before serving. Cumin also comes in powdered form.

Garlic
One of the oldest herbs in the world, it must be carefully handled. For best results, press or crush garlic clove.

Marjoram
An aromatic herb of the mint family, it is good in soups, sauces, stuffings and stews.

Mustard (dry)
Brings a sharp bite to sauces. Sprinkle just a touch over roast chicken for a delightful flavor treat.

Oregano
A staple herb in Italian, Spanish and Mexican cuisines. It is very good in dishes with a tomato foundation; it adds an excellent savory taste.

Paprika	A mild pepper that adds color to many dishes. The very best paprika is imported from Hungary.
Rosemary	A tasty herb important in seasoning stuffing for duck, partridge, capon and other poultry.
Sage	A perennial favorite with all kinds of poultry and stuffings. It is particularly good with goose.
Tarragon	One of the *fines herbes*. Goes well with all poultry dishes whether hot or cold.
Thyme	Usually used in combination with bay leaf in soups, stews and sauces.

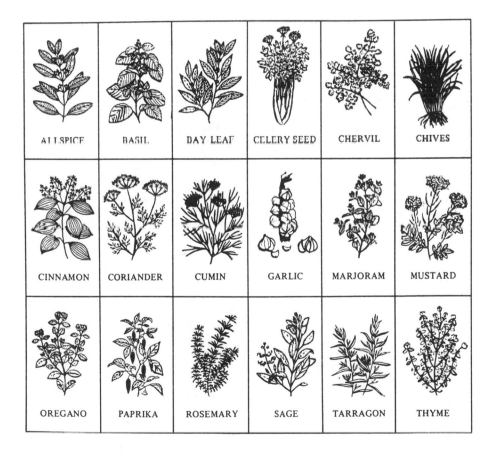

INDEX

You may order as many *New England Pioneer Pantry* cookbooks as you wish for the price of **$10.00** each plus **$2.50** postage and handling per book ordered. Mail form and check for **$12.50** for each cookbook ordered to:

**Merrimack Valley Works Chapter #78
Telephone Pioneers of America
1600 Osgood Street
North Andover, Massachusetts 01845**

Number of Cookbooks Ordered: _____

Check Enclosed for Amount of: _____

**Please Make Checks Payable To:
Merrimack Valley Works Chapter #78, TPA**

Ship To:

Name: _____

Address: _____

City, State, Zip: _____

Daytime Telephone Number: (_____) _____

Order a book for a friend and we'll ship it direct.

Ship To:

Name: _____

Address: _____

City, State, Zip: _____

Daytime Telephone Number: (_____) _____